Ready or Not

The Bridegroom
IS
RETURNING

There Will be a Rapture

Ready or Not

The Bridegroom IS RETURNING

There Will be a Rapture

Michael Hunter

Published by

First Page Solutions
Kelowna, BC, Canada

PREFACE

    Please do not skip over the Bible quotations dispersed throughout this book. The Scriptures are not there to help support the opinions of this book or its author. The purpose of this book is to help the reader become more familiar with the Word of God. We cannot learn to love God's Word if we do not read it. Many of the Scriptures have been taken from the King James Version of the Bible because I have found it to generally be the most commonly available accurate translation of the original Hebrew and Greek manuscripts.

    I did keep in mind, however, that the King James Version of the Bible was written hundreds of years ago and contains many words and phrases that are now no longer in common usage. Therefore, for the purpose of clarity and ease of understanding, you will find that some passages are paraphrased (contain modern language) in order to help explain antiquated words and phrases. In doing this, every effort has been made to make certain that such paraphrases retain the integrity of the original Greek and Hebrew in order to ensure that nothing is added to or taken away from God's Word.

There are also numerous Bible quotes throughout this book that are taken from several other translations of the Bible simply because I believe that they offer the clearest and most accurate modern language translation of that particular passage, expressing the Word of God in a way that is easy for everyone to understand while maintaining the integrity of the original Hebrew and Greek Scriptures. Greek and Hebrew definitions have been sourced from Strong's Exhaustive Concordance.

Scripture quotations have all been taken from the online Bible Search website "Bible Gateway" https://www.biblegateway.com as per the following information:

DEDICATION

I want to express my gratitude to my wonderful and beautiful wife of many years, Leigh Ann and also to my good friend Diane for their help in proofreading and editing this book. I pray the Lord blesses you both for your willing hearts to reach people for Jesus.

CONTENTS

INTRODUCTION

The "resurrection" of Christian believers (also known as the "Rapture," the "catching up" of the Bride of Christ, and the "return of Christ for His body-the church") at Father God's appointed time has always been a foundational belief of Christianity. Yet, it is a Biblical doctrine which has been challenged right from the very beginning by those who do not believe. Even when Jesus was walking around Israel telling people that He would be resurrected on the third day, the Sadducees were already contradicting what Jesus was saying, claiming there is no resurrection, so I ask you this question. "Who are we to believe when it comes to the Rapture and Resurrection?"

Let not your heart be troubled: ye believe in God, believe also in me. In my Father's house are many mansions: if it were not so, I would have told you. I go to prepare a place for you. And if I go and prepare a place for you, I WILL come again, and receive you unto myself; that where I AM, there ye may be also. John 14:1-3 KJV

Later, when the Apostle Paul said "Why are you saying there is no resurrection?" Paul was referring to both Christ's resurrection and OUR resurrection:

But tell me this—since we preach that Christ rose from the dead, why are some of you saying there will be no resurrection of the dead? For if there is no resurrection of the dead, then Christ has not been raised either. And if Christ has not been raised, then all our preaching is useless, and your faith is useless. 1 Corinthians 15:12-15 NLT

Then, through the Apostle Paul, God goes on to point out that our very salvation is linked to resurrection:

And if there is no resurrection of the dead, then Christ has not been raised. And if Christ has not been raised, then your faith is useless and you are still guilty of your sins. In that case, all who have died believing in Christ are lost! And if our hope in Christ is only for this life, we are more to be pitied than anyone in the world. But in fact, Christ has been raised from the dead. He is the first of a great harvest of all who have died. 1 Corinthians 15:16-20 NLT

Jesus Christ has indeed been resurrected from the dead, just as He said it would occur. However, His resurrection was just the first half of the fulfilment of Christ's promise to His disciples. This book is focused on the soon-coming fulfilment of the SECOND half of the promise Jesus Christ made to His followers after they had become deeply troubled by His warnings that He was about to be taken from them, tortured and murdered.

Namely, God has placed it in my heart to strongly encourage every reader to have hope and believe our Lord will return as He said He would, and when He does, there WILL be a rapture/resurrection of both the living and deceased who have repented and believed on Jesus Christ for salvation.

Chapter 1

Does God Exist?

Is the Bible True?

Is there a God? Are the things that are written in the Bible true? Or are they just stories invented through the imaginations of men? The Scriptures tell us that man never "evolved" from some mentally deficient ancestor of the apes. The Bible declares God is the Creator of the entire material universe, including man and all other life on Earth. Is it true? Is it just wishful thinking? Or maybe it's all just some elaborate lie?

There is only one man in human history who can prove or disprove whether the Bible is the Word of God and whether or not we will be resurrected, and that man is Jesus Christ. Paul the Apostle said that if there is no resurrection, then Jesus Christ has not risen from the dead. If that was true, all of those who claim to have seen Him resurrected would be liars, and Christianity is in vain and the faith of everyone who believes in the Bible and Jesus Christ is in vain, so what point would there be in promoting and being willing to die for God and Christianity if it is all a lie?

Yet, is the Bible a lie? If it is a lie, then it is the most effective and successful lie ever told, for the message of Jesus Christ's resurrection from the dead to become the Savior of all who believe Him and follow Him started with only 12 men and a few women about two thousand years ago, and now it has become the largest spiritual religious movement on the whole planet, with over 2 billion followers claiming to believe in Jesus Christ as mankind's Savior. We must remember however, Jesus Himself stated that not everyone who claimed to believe in God and Christ would be going WITH Him when He returns to this Earth.

This book is primarily about the return of Jesus to "catch up" His Bride before the wrath of God falls upon this end-times wicked and adulterous generation of humanity. Yet, before we address that specific event, it is important to do the groundwork and give readers a firm foundation in who Jesus said WILL be going with Him when He comes for His Bride.

Everyone today wants to know the day and hour when Jesus will return, but many in these last days have stopped their ears to God's warnings that not all who claim to know God and Jesus will be going with Jesus when He returns for His Bride. In fact, God declares that there will even be many who are RELIGIOUS and proclaiming that Jesus is Lord and watching for His return. Yet these same people will be staying behind with the rest of the unrepentant majority of humanity to endure God's seven years of wrath.

Why? One of the primary problems with this end-times generation is that most people today want to be told that they will be saved from the punishment of the Tribulation and hell, but they do not really want a Savior from their sin. They have no real desire to be delivered from their iniquities and evil behaviors, in spite of God's warnings that evil will not dwell with Him. They ignore God pleading to us in His Word, not only calling to the nation of Israel, but to the Gentiles (all other people on Earth) as well, declaring:

Say to them, 'As surely as I live, declares the Sovereign Lord, I take no pleasure in the death of the wicked, but rather that they turn from their ways and live. Turn! Turn from your evil ways! Why will you die, people of Israel?' Ezekiel 33:11 NIV

So, when IS Jesus coming? About six thousand years have passed since God told Adam and Eve that He would one day send mankind a Redeemer who would be born of the seed of one of Eve's descendants, and God promised that this Redeemer would crush Satan and his hold over humanity, but it still hasn't happened yet.

Does that mean that God has forgotten the human race? No! God declares that He will still fulfill all of His promises at His appointed times. God has already fulfilled the first part of His promise. He has already sent us our Redeemer, His Son Jesus Christ.

We also know from the Scriptures and from secular history that it has been almost two thousand years since Jesus left this Earth, and before He left, Jesus explained to His followers that He was going to His Father's House to prepare a place for us, saying that one day He would return for us, to "catch us up" and take us to our mansions in His Father's House where HE IS, and from that time on, Jesus promised that we will continue to be WITH Him forever.

Don't let your hearts be troubled. Trust in God, and trust also in me. There is more than enough room in my Father's home. If this were not so, would I have told you that I am going to prepare a place for you? When everything is ready, I will come and get you, so that you will always be with me where I am. John 14:1-3 NLT

Okay! Okay! But, if it is all true, when is it going to happen? It's been six thousand years since Adam and Eve, and two thousand years since Jesus was killed and supposedly resurrected. How much longer is it going to be, already? When is Jesus coming back? Where's the proof that the Bible is true?

Does it surprise you that the Scriptures tell us that God knew (and even said) that people in the end times would be asking these kinds of questions, particularly people who don't want to hear or know the truth, and are just looking for excuses not to change their evil lifestyles and behavior?

Dear friends, this is now my second letter to you. I have written both of them as reminders to stimulate you to wholesome thinking. I want you to recall the words spoken in the past by the holy prophets and the command given by our Lord and Savior through your apostles. Above all, you must understand that in the last days scoffers will come, scoffing and following their own evil desires. They will say, "Where is this 'coming' he promised? Ever since our ancestors died, everything goes on as it has since the beginning of creation." But they deliberately forget that long ago by God's word the heavens came into being and the earth was formed out of water and by water. By these waters also the world of that time was deluged and destroyed. By the same word the present heavens and earth are reserved for fire, being kept for the Day of Judgment and destruction of the ungodly. 2 Peter 3:1-7 NIV

Yes, dear friends. There is a day of judgement coming for the ungodly, for those who prefer evil to good, and darkness to light. So, what kind of God does that make the God of the Bible? Is God a cruel taskmaster who wants to destroy mankind just because they do not follow Him? Hardly!

If you take the time to study all of the things that will be happening during the Tribulation, you will discover that most of the evil that comes upon humanity will come from mankind's own wickedness and their insistence to blindly and ignorantly follow the Devil without realizing that it is SATAN'S agenda and goal to kill as many human beings as he can during the Tribulation in order to continue to subjugate them to himself in hell and the Lake of Fire forever.

Don't ever get it in your mind that God wants to send people to hell. Neither does God want to destroy mankind during the Tribulation. On the contrary, in God's mercy, He has given humanity ample time to repent. The Lord has given mankind thousands of years of grace since the world was first destroyed in Noah's day.

It has always been God's desire that we would all change our evil ways and not have to go through the worst period of history that mankind will ever have to endure, a time which will culminate in more focused and intense suffering than the human race has ever seen, or will ever see again.

Many people today have not really grasped that the coming Tribulation is an ordeal of unimaginable horror that would definitely end with the extinction of humanity if Jesus does not return to put a stop to this insanity of man's continuing pursuit of the knowledge of evil.

For then there will be great tribulation, such as has not been since the beginning of the world until this time, no, nor ever shall be. And unless those days were shortened, no flesh would be saved; but for the elect's sake those days will be shortened. Matthew 24:21-22 NKJV

I have a question for those who teach that the Bride of Christ will be going through the Tribulation: "What kind of Ogre do you think God is?" God has never wanted man to experience evil. He did not want it for Adam and Eve. He did not want it for Israel, and He does not want it for the church. God does not want anyone presently living to go through the Tribulation, let alone the beloved Bride of His only Son, Jesus. Yet, all who continue to reject God and follow the Devil WILL go through the Tribulation.

But do not forget this one thing, dear friends: With the Lord a day is like a thousand years, and a thousand years are like a day. The Lord is not slow in keeping his promise, as some understand slowness. Instead he is patient with you, not wanting anyone to perish, but everyone to come to repentance. 2 Peter 3:8-9 NIV

Listen, dear friends, just because Christians have suffered persecution ever since the church was founded, those who do not really know God's loving heart have mistakenly gotten it in their minds that persecution is part of God's plan for salvation. They think that the Lord deliberately designed the coming Seven Year Tribulation to be God's "torture" test for the Bride of Christ to prove that we are worthy to go with Jesus when He arrives at the end to set up His kingdom on Earth as it is in Heaven. However, that is not what is taught in the Bible and I do not believe that those who think in this way have an accurate understanding of how much God really loves us.

The Lord says in His Word that the "Law" and the penalties for breaking the law are not for the righteous, but for the wicked. Likewise, God also makes it clear to us that the anger and wrath of God that will be poured out upon the unrepentant of humanity during the last seven years of Satan's rule over mankind (the Tribulation) are not reserved for those made righteous by repentance, God's grace, and faith in Jesus Christ. The Tribulation is designed for the wicked, those who love darkness and are unrepentant, calling evil good, and good evil.

Nonetheless, when those who are presently the enemies of God, go through the Tribulation, it will not happen because God hates them and takes delight in punishing and killing everyone. That is simply not the heart and Spirit of God.

Rather, it has always been God's greatest desire that once the wicked have experienced the horrors of living under Satan's rule rather than God's goodness, they will humble themselves, repent and come back to their true Father in Heaven again, just as described in the story of the prodigal son in Luke 15:10-22, and also in 2 Chronicles:

If my people, which are called by my name, shall humble themselves, and pray, and seek my face, and turn from their wicked ways; then will I hear from heaven, and will forgive their sin, and will heal their land. 2 Chronicles 7:14 KJV

Really, God's record of grace, forgiveness, mercy and redemption is clearly recorded throughout the whole history of mankind and the nation of Israel. Unrepentant sin is the reason why God destroyed the world in Noah's day. It is the reason God permitted Israel to be defeated and taken into captivity, and so it will also be for all humanity during the last seven years of Satan's wrath-filled rule on Earth.

God does not WANT mankind to suffer through such a time of evil. Rather, it is God's deepest desire that (during that time) at least some will turn from their wicked ways, come back to God and be saved. Once mankind realizes just how horrible it is to live in a world where the Antichrist and Satan are going to rule for seven years with almost no restraint to the evil they do and influence man to do, it is God's will that, perhaps then they will repent and return to their Father in Heaven who loves them.

How Can We Know God Exists?

I would venture to say that, "Is there a God?" is by far the most important question in the world today with relation to human existence and how we should live our lives. It is certainly a question that most of us have struggled with at some point in our lives. Does God even exist? Yet, when it comes down to one's personal life and death, the truth is that there are very few genuine atheists in the world, and God tells us in His Word that there are some sound logical reasons for that.

But God shows his anger from heaven against all sinful, wicked people who suppress the truth by their wickedness. They know the truth about God because he has made it obvious to them. For ever since the world was created, people have seen the earth and sky. Through everything God made, they can clearly see his invisible qualities—his eternal power and divine nature. So they have no excuse for not knowing God. Romans 1:18-20 NLT

Yes, in His own Word, God states that sinful people suppress the truth by their wickedness. They can clearly see God's invisible qualities by the things God has created, and therefore they have no excuse for not believing God exists, or not wanting to know God. The Lord also says that (through faith) we CAN know that God created us, the Earth, and the rest of the universe, and that everything is held together by His invisible power.

By faith we understand that the universe was formed at God's command, so that what is seen was not made out of what was visible. Hebrews 11:3 NIV

And it is impossible to please God without faith. Anyone who wants to come to him must believe that God exists and that he rewards those who sincerely seek him. Hebrews 11:6 NLT

He is the God who made the world and everything in

it. Since he is Lord of heaven and earth, he doesn't live in man-made temples, and human hands can't serve his needs—for he has no needs. He himself gives life and breath to everything, and he satisfies every need. From one man he created all the nations throughout the whole earth. He decided beforehand when they should rise and fall, and he determined their boundaries. His purpose was for the nations to seek after God and perhaps feel their way toward him and find him—though he is not far from any one of us. For in him we live and move and exist. As some of your own poets have said, 'We are his offspring.' And since this is true, we shouldn't think of God as an idol designed by craftsmen from gold or silver or stone. Acts 17:24-29 NLT

From here, God then also says in the book of Acts that He overlooked mankind's ignorance of such things in ancient times, but now, in these last days, we have more than enough evidence to determine that what God says is true because of the resurrection of Jesus Christ, and yet there are still those who mock and doubt God, putting off believing the truth, while demanding more supernatural "signs." They always want more proof before they will believe and turn from their evil ways:

God overlooked people's ignorance about these things in earlier times, but now he commands everyone everywhere to repent of their sins and turn to him. For he has set a day for judging the world with justice by the man he has appointed, and he proved to everyone who this is by raising him from the dead. When they heard Paul speak about the resurrection of the dead, some laughed in contempt, but others said, "We want to hear more about this later." Acts 17:30-32 NLT

In addition, God declares in the Holy Scriptures that we can actually know by FAITH that it was Jesus Christ in His original form as the "WORD" (who was God and is God) who created the material universe and everything in it. This present universe did not just "explode" randomly into existence by itself as the atheistic "big bang" theory claims. From the very beginning, God (The Father, The Word, and The Holy Spirit) was the Creator of all that exists in the material universe.

In the beginning the Word already existed. The Word was with God, and the Word was God. He existed in the beginning with God. God created everything through him, and nothing was created except through him. The Word gave life to everything that was created. John 1:1-4 NLT

He came into the very world he created, but the world didn't recognize him. He came to his own people, and even they rejected him. But to all who believed him and accepted him, he gave the right to become children of God. They are reborn—not with a physical birth resulting from human passion or plan, but a birth that comes from God. So the Word became human and made his home among us. He was full of unfailing love and faithfulness. And we have seen his glory, the glory of the Father's one and only Son. John 1:10-14 NLT

So the truth is that even though Father God in Heaven is presently invisible to our natural eyes, God can still be found and known by those who really want to know and form a relationship with Him through the exercising of our faith. The Scriptures have revealed to us that if we really want to see God, we can SEE Him through the life of His Son Jesus Christ, through God's inspired Word, the Bible, and through everything that God has created.

Yet, one of the great tragedies of modern religion is that most people today still doubt (or only have a vague idea) that God exists. Others believe that God loves us and Jesus is the Son of God and God's chosen Savior of humanity, and that is about as far as their version of the path to salvation goes. Why? It is because it costs humanity very little (almost nothing) to believe that much. In fact, God even tells us in His Word that the devils know and believe that God and Jesus exist. Yet, they will still end up in the Lake of Fire. Why? Because their ways are evil continuously and they refuse to turn from their evil thoughts and deeds to walk in GOD'S ways, and the Lord says that all who follow them in this life will also follow them to their final destination after death.

Chapter 2

Believe In God? Or Believe God?

Believing In God Did Not Save Adam!

It is important to realize, dear friends, there is a huge difference between believing IN God (believing God exists) and BELIEVING God (believing what God has to say to us in His Word).

Over 2 billion people around the world in this end-times generation claim to believe in God and Jesus Christ. Yet, most of this last days generation of humanity (including many professing Christians) still refuse to believe what God and Jesus Christ have to say to us in the Holy Bible regarding God's only way to salvation, through repentance and faith in Jesus Christ.

That is the world's most serious problem in these last days. Most people are not avowed atheists. They believe IN God, and yet they do not BELIEVE God. Furthermore, there are so many preachers and teachers spouting unbiblical beliefs about God in these end times that many are just continuing along the broad path of sin and unrepentance toward hell and the Lake of Fire and they don't even know it.

It is actually the exact same mistake that Adam and Eve made in the Garden of Eden. Adam and Eve believed IN God. In fact they KNEW God existed. They knew God personally, walking and talking with God, the Word who created them, but they still chose not to believe what God had to say to them. They listened instead to the deceiver (the Devil), and as a result of that false belief, evil entered their being, and now evil and death exist on Earth, where once there was only the goodness of God and the potential for eternal life for mankind.

In short, Adam and Eve are the proof to us that believing IN God (believing there is a God) is where we need to start if we want to come to God, but it is not enough for salvation. It is no guarantee of salvation. Even the devils believe in God and tremble with fear. Believing IN God is only the first step toward salvation.

I Too Believed in God

As a child growing up in a dysfunctional family marked by PTSD, alcohol abuse, depression and violence, I deeply questioned the existence of God in my early years. My parents were not married and there was violence in our home. Yet, my mom and dad expressed a nominal faith in God's existence, even attending a local church fairly regularly until my dad suddenly died of a stroke when I was only four years old.

The only cemetery in the small community was owned by that church, and although my parents had been welcomed at the church and their donations had been welcome in the offering plate, the local church was not willing to show mercy to a grieving widow with a small child and bury a "sinner" in their cemetery.

Since that was the only cemetery in the whole community, Mom had to have Dad's body shipped out to a larger city for a civic burial. Needless to say, those circumstances surrounding Dad's death created a rift between Mom and local churches that would last for many years.

Shortly after my biological father died, Mom did marry another man and this man adopted me and became my stepfather. Unfortunately, he was even less religious than my natural father, and an alcoholic to boot. As a result, I grew up with very little understanding of God, or faith in God. In fact I had a lot of resentment toward both parents (who fought a lot), and toward God (whom I was not completely convinced even existed at that point in my life).

However, I was fortunate enough to grow up in the 1950's when society pretty well still shut down on Sundays to give people the opportunity to attend church and spend time with their families.

Even though my parents did not regularly attend church themselves, like a lot of other nominal professing Christians, they did find another church in a different town. There, they sent me to Sunday school, and sometimes they showed up themselves on religious holidays or when I was involved in some sort of special kids' church presentation.

So I did get some teaching from a Protestant Sunday School about Jesus loving me and dying for my sins when I was younger. I liked the idea of that, but the life I experienced at home was far from the teachings of Jesus in the Bible, and this, combined with the normal trials and tribulations of life growing up created a lot of doubt in my mind about the existence of God and the real value of Christianity.

Neither did it help things at all when I hit my teens in the 1960's and early 70's during the years when teaching the theories of evolution was becoming popular in schools. It was a time when a lot of scientists and educators were really beginning to take aim at and make efforts to mock, deny and disprove the existence of God and the inspiration and authenticity of the Bible.

Not only that, those were the decades of the explosion of recreational drug use in Canada and the re-defining of the morals and sexual values of society, which were all drifting further and further from the Biblical behavioral pattern laid out for us by God in the Bible. Much of that which is called "evil" in the Word of God was being relabeled as "free love", "alternate lifestyle" and becoming an acceptable level of behavior in modern society.

Then, to top off all those other negative influences, in school (and later on in adult life) I kept running into many people in society who claimed to be Christians, yet they did not at all live their lives according to the Bible. Their daily lives and behavior were not much different than that of people of other religions or those who claimed they did not believe in God at all. Sadly, in some cases, the behavior of those who claimed to be Christians was even worse, more sinful than unbelievers or those of other religions (who were sometimes much nicer people).

Another part of the problem when I was growing up was that there was a prevailing belief among professing Christians (and it still persists today) that all you had to do was say "I believe in Jesus" and it met God's requirements to make you a Christian "guaranteed" for heaven, regardless of how wickedly a person lives for the rest of their daily life.

Therefore, like many others who are unlearned and don't know any better, I bought into that lie. Intellectually, I came to the conclusion that God existed and Jesus died to save us, and I decided to "believe in" God and called myself a Christian, comparing myself to others who claimed to be Christian and thinking to myself that everybody sins, and my sins may be worse than some, but they are not as bad as those of others who say they are Christians.

My philosophy in those days was "If they're going to make it to Heaven, so am I." I did not like to think about the idea that maybe many of us who claimed to be Christians back then would not be going with Jesus at all when He returns for those who truly love Him.

I understand now what a big mistake that was. It was a FALSE belief system, and in the end it cost me my family, my job, my reputation, my wealth, my mental stability and even my freedom (eventually ending up in maximum security prison for a time as a result of my continued sinning). Yet, I still kept going in the same evil and sinful direction away from God until I reached the absolute bottom.

Even worse than that, those false beliefs almost cost me my life as a result of an oppressive evil spirit which began to influence me for a time toward committing suicide. In the end, I found out the hard way that (without a proper understanding of God and Jesus Christ) there was no hope for me to be truly happy in this life, and it was only by the mercy of God that Satan did not completely destroy me. In fact, the truth is that there is no hope for the rest of humanity who keep rejecting God either.

I am no pessimist. I am a realist. All we have to do is look around us to see that (in spite of all of our religion, all of our knowledge, and our advances in technology) our ever-increasing knowledge of good and evil isn't saving us at all.

In spite of all our increased technology and accumulated knowledge, our world is not getting better as humanity in general gets further and further from God. It is clear to those who are paying attention that even our planet itself is rapidly deteriorating ecologically. The Earth is losing its ability to sustain life, slowly being overrun by human habitation and suffocating in an overspreading of garbage, pollution and a destruction of the environment.

Human society itself is no different. In general, mankind is becoming ever more spiritually, morally, politically, and economically corrupted as we draw ever closer to what the Bible refers to as the seven year Tribulation and Armageddon (WWIII), which God declares will put an end to all life on Earth if God Himself does not put a stop to it by sending Jesus to take over.

Even the "space race" is not really fueled by curiosity and exploration. Their motivation for spending trillions of dollars on this venture is about the intellectual elite of society comprehending that we are a self-serving race of beings living on a dying planet.

They know that (unless the God that they don't believe in intervenes) the only other viable option for mankind's survival will be if we are able to expand out into the galaxy before our corrupted and destructive presence on Earth becomes the cause of the complete ruination and destruction of our planet, and ends in our own self-extinction.

Furthermore, an additional problem which we have is

that the scientists (and those who govern this world) already know from the evidence that we are running out of time to be able to make this transition to other planets happen soon enough. They just won't be able to make it happen in time.

This means that (by their line of thinking) the only other alternative for man's future survival will be that government will eventually need to begin utilizing the evil of "culling" the human population to ensure that those with wealth and power and an allegiance to their common causes will be able to continue to survive, dominate and control the world population on Earth until safe space travel to other planets can be achieved.

How does all of this relate to God and the Bible? It means that the human race is in real trouble. The seven years of Tribulation and Armageddon (World War III) spoken of in the Bible as occurring during the "end times" is almost upon us. We need to start looking at world events and realize that NOW is the time for each of us individually to turn around and start following Christ if we are not already doing so. Jesus warned His disciples:

Now learn a lesson from the fig tree. When its branches bud and its leaves begin to sprout, you know that summer is near. In the same way, when you see all these things taking place, you can know that his return is very near, right at the door. Mark 13:28-29 NLT

Yet in the midst of all these uncertain and perilous times, God has promised in His Word that at the midnight hour of the last days of the end times there exists a "blessed hope" for all who truly believe God and have faith in Jesus Christ.

We can be confident in Christ's promise that He will come again to "catch up" those who love and follow Him. He will receive us unto Himself so that WHERE HE NOW IS, we may be also, and so shall we ever be with the Lord. Therefore, for those who are already Christians, we should be encouraged and comforted by these words.

God is Real! The Bible is True!

If there is no God, then the Bible is full of lies and it is nothing more than the ideas and philosophies of the men and women who wrote it. However, if (as the Bible itself proclaims) the Scriptures are inspired by God, I would say that it is of utmost importance to our eternal destiny to both know and BELIEVE what God is saying to us, and then live our lives accordingly in these end times:

But you must remain faithful to the things you have been taught. You know they are true, for you know you can trust those who taught you. You have been taught the Holy Scriptures from childhood, and they have given you the wisdom to receive the salvation that comes by trusting in Christ Jesus. All Scripture is inspired by God and is useful to teach us what is true and to make us realize what is wrong in our lives. It corrects us when we are wrong and teaches us to do what is right. God uses it to prepare and equip his people to do every good work. 2 Timothy 3:14-17 NLT

For we were not making up clever stories when we told

you about the powerful coming of our Lord Jesus Christ. We saw his majestic splendor with our own eyes when he received honor and glory from God the Father. The voice from the majestic glory of God said to him, "This is my dearly loved Son, who brings me great joy." We ourselves heard that voice from heaven when we were with him on the holy mountain. Because of that experience, we have even greater confidence in the message proclaimed by the prophets. You must pay close attention to what they wrote, for their words are like a lamp shining in a dark place—until the Day dawns, and Christ the Morning Star shines in your hearts. Above all, you must realize that no prophecy in Scripture ever came from the prophet's own understanding, or from human initiative. No, those prophets were moved by the Holy Spirit, and they spoke from God. 2 Peter 1:16-21 NLT

What about Jesus Christ? The Holy Bible details the most astounding claims about Him and records Jesus making some of the most amazing promises in human history, and many of those promises have already come true.

In no more time than about 2,000 years since the inception of the Christian church on the day of Pentecost (beginning with only a handful of believers in the tiny nation of Israel), Christianity has grown to be the largest religion in the world with more than 2 billion people claiming to believe in God and in Jesus Christ as mankind's Savior. Either the Bible and Christianity is the biggest single deception in human history, or it is the truth, and we would be wise to believe what Jesus taught.

If Christianity is a deception, then it is certainly the most massive lie in human history. Yet, what if the one-quarter of modern mankind who believe in God, in Heaven and Hell, and Jesus Christ as God's Son are the ones who have found the truth, and it is the rest of society who are the ones who are deceived and headed for a lost eternity? Have you ever thought about that?

What if, in corporate humanity's continuous quest for knowledge, most have become deceived by their own evil and their own vanities? What if (as the Bible says) by ignoring God's inspired Word, and thinking themselves to be wise, the majority of humanity have become fools?

God says in the Bible that more and more people in the last days will fall to the delusion of believing that the atheists and evolutionists are telling the truth. They will believe there is no God "as He is described in the Bible."

The reality is that many today have lost their faith in the one true God and follow unknown gods of their own lustful desires and their vain imaginations. They believe in other gods, demonic gods whom they imagine are no more than alien beings more evolved than we are, and suppose we even have a common ancestor.

Therefore, they say there is no need for us to live our lives in obedience to what God has to say to us in the Bible because they are convinced that the Bible is irrelevant to modern society. Yet, God does not mince words when He talks about those who have rejected Him.

Yes, they knew God, but they wouldn't worship him as God or even give him thanks. And they began to think up foolish ideas of what God was like. As a result, their minds became dark and confused. Claiming to be wise, they instead became utter fools. Romans 1:21-22 NLT

Furthermore, God declares in His Word that "in the last days" as society becomes even more corrupted, flawed and deficient, the "knowledge of evil" which Adam and Eve chose to become part of our being will become an ever-increasing problem for mankind, driving the human race in general further and further from the truth as they become ever more corrupted by evil.

We have certainly seen this happening in the last few decades as many (but not all) in the scientific and medical community, our educators, and our political leaders in our country have been abandoning the Biblical testimony of who God is and what He desires of us.

In their unbelief, they have turned to establishing their own moral and spiritual standards for society that are decidedly anti-Christ. In addition, more than a few professing Christians have degenerated to the state of promoting their own concepts of Christianity based on their own ungodly lifestyles and corrupted notions of God.

You should know this, Timothy that in the last days there will be very difficult times. For people will love only themselves and their money. They will be boastful and proud, scoffing at God, disobedient to their parents, and ungrateful. They will consider nothing sacred. They will be unloving and unforgiving; they will slander others and have no self-control. They will be cruel and hate what is good. They will betray their friends, be reckless, be puffed up with pride, and love pleasure rather than God. They will act religious, but they will reject the power that could make them godly. Stay away from people like that! They are the kind who work their way into people's homes and win the confidence of vulnerable women who are burdened with the guilt of sin and controlled by various desires. (Such women are forever following new teachings, but they are never able to understand the truth.) These teachers oppose the truth just as Jannes and Jambres opposed Moses. They have depraved minds and a counterfeit faith. 2 Timothy 3:1-8 NLT

God Must be Spiritually Discerned

One important thing that the Bible says about God is that the Lord cannot be discovered and known through human intellect alone. As a young man, I can honestly say that I was intellectually smarter than many people. I dropped out of high school due to the dysfunction in our family, but went back ten years later and graduated with a 96 percentile average. So, I had the intellect to know that something is seriously wrong with humanity, and maybe what the Bible said about God was true.

Through taking tests around that time, I discovered I had a MENSA level I.Q. Yet, it did not save me. If anything, my intellect was a hindrance to me. I was a voracious reader. I studied numerous religions and read the Bible many times over, but my accumulated knowledge and human wisdom was never enough to enable me to grasp who God really is, because even the most intelligent and educated and powerful people in the world are nothing in comparison to the omniscience, omnipresence, and omnipotence of God.

I was never able to find the truth until much later in life when (through faith) I finally realized God can be found just as easily by a small child or simple fisherman as He can by a doctor, lawyer or scientist.

Over the years, I have learned to humbly admit that there are things about God that are simply beyond our present comprehension in the natural realm, and no matter how smart we think we are, some things can only be spiritually discerned. They can only be known by our exercise of faith and trust in God and His love for us.

Even right from the very beginning, Adam and Eve made the fatal mistake of trying to use their intellect alone to discern the truth instead of using their faith to believe, trust, and obey the God who created them.

Adam and Eve could have remained in the safety of being part of God's family FOREVER by eating from the tree of life instead of the tree of knowledge of good and evil. All they had to do was to continue to believe, trust, and obey God, but they chose instead to reject God and believe Satan. They adopted Satan as their leader and father, giving the Devil dominion over them; and look how that has turned out for the human race.

Nonetheless, the Bible tells each one of us that if we will just take that first step of faith to BELIEVE that God exists and is a rewarder of those who are sincerely looking for Him, this pleases God and He WILL reward us for earnestly seeking Him.

Now faith is confidence in what we hope for and assurance about what we do not see. This is what the ancients were commended for. Hebrews 11:1-2 NIV

And it is impossible to please God without faith. Anyone

who wants to come to him must believe that God exists and that he rewards those who sincerely seek him. Hebrews 11:6 NIV

So, how does God reward those who earnestly seek Him? God's promise to us is that if we want to receive the knowledge of God, He will send His own Spirit to help us learn of Him and guide us toward all truth. The whole purpose of Jesus sending the Holy Spirit was to have us receive Him within our being and He would teach us about God and His ways from within. God's Word says:

Nevertheless I tell you the truth. It is to your advantage that I go away; for if I do not go away, the Helper will not come to you; but if I depart, I will send Him to you. John 16:7 NKJV

However, when He, the Spirit of truth, has come, He will guide you into all truth; for He will not speak on His own *authority,* but whatever He hears He will speak; and He will tell you things to come. John 16:13 NKJV

That is what the Scriptures mean when they say, "No eye has seen, no ear has heard, and no mind has imagined what God has prepared for those who love him." But it was to us that God revealed these things by his Spirit. For his Spirit searches out everything and shows us God's deep secrets. No one can know a person's thoughts except that person's own spirit, and no one can know God's thoughts except God's own Spirit. And we have received God's Spirit (not the world's spirit), so we can know the wonderful things God has freely given us. When we tell you these things, we do not use words that come from human wisdom. Instead, we speak words given to us by the Spirit, using the Spirit's words to explain spiritual truths. But people who aren't spiritual can't receive these truths from God's Spirit. It all sounds foolish to them and they can't understand it, for only those who are spiritual can understand what the Spirit means. 1 Corinthians 2:9-14 NLT

That is exactly the way it was for me, dear friends. In the natural, I am an intelligent man. I was intelligent enough to believe that God exists, but all of my intellectual knowledge was not enough to help me understand God or why God wanted me to change my behavior and walk in daily obedience to Him. I was one of those people God describes in Matthew:

These people honor me with their lips, but their hearts are far from me. Mathew 15:8 NLT

The end result of my spiritually dead works as a young man was that, even though I **thought** I had taken the right steps to become a Christian, and I claimed to be a Christian, and I did a lot of the "religious" things that Christians do, I did not really know God or His Word back then, and my sin almost destroyed me.

There was no real love relationship between myself and Jesus. I was not really a follower of Jesus Christ, and the only thing my efforts to live an "unbiblical" Christianity accomplished was to produce a corrupted life that had no real firm foundation in God and was doomed to fail when trials and tribulations came.

My original beliefs about God were like a house with no foundation, built on sand, and when the trials of life came along, the whole thing collapsed. It was only when I was at the very lowest point in my life and I finally began to cry out to God in my tiny faith, really hoping He was out there somewhere and He could hear me that THEN, my life suddenly changed.

When I finally came to God in humility, bawling my eyes out, admitting to my Father in Heaven that it was not His fault that my life was a disaster, God was listening. The reality was that I knew my life was a mess because I had not been truly obeying God or living for Him. I was just unwilling to admit it until then. When I was finally ready to be honest with God, the Lord heard me, had compassion on me, and His Holy Spirit helped guide me out of the pit I had gotten myself into.

On that wonderful, life-changing day when I finally acknowledged to God that I had not really believed, trusted and obeyed Him - when I cried out to God that I could not go on living like this anymore and I desperately needed to be saved and have His Holy Spirit dwelling inside of me to help me change my life - something SUPERNATURAL happened, something that no words which I could ever write in these pages can ever fully explain to any reader.

The presence of God's grace, and His love, and His mercy, and His forgiveness began to fill the car I was sitting in until I could no longer sit up anymore and the weight and power of God's loving presence drove me to the floor of the vehicle, where I lay wailing in godly sorrow, unable to move under the weight of the Spirit of God.

There I lay, pinned to the floor by the presence of God's Spirit, groaning and sobbing in repentance for the longest time, and yet at the same time feeling the weight of my sin being lifted off of me until God's presence gradually receded. Right there, for the first time in my life, I finally KNEW that God is real.

From that day forward in my life there has never been a single moment in time since then that I have ever, ever doubted that God is real and that He cares about me and loves me deeply and personally. Even though that event occurred 40 years ago, and I have never had an identical experience since then, the memory and the glory of God's presence and goodness on that day was so wonderful that it is just as real today as if it happened this morning, and my life has never been the same since then.

Until that important day in my life, I never really understood (even after many years of studying the Bible and church attendance and telling people that I believed in God and Jesus) that I had only come to an intellectual conclusion that God was real, but I had never KNOWN God in a personal way. That kind of knowledge only comes to human beings through communicating with God spirit to Spirit.

Before that day, I only had a vague concept that there was a God and that the Bible was probably true. In my mind, I had come to the intellectual conclusion that God existed and Jesus was the Savior. At least I hoped the Bible was true, yet I had still been continuing in my wicked ways because I had been lied to and I didn't really know any better.

Much of the preaching I had heard was enough to convince me to go up to an altar as a young man and publicly profess to believe in God and Jesus. It was enough to motivate me to attend a local church and be baptized, but it was never clear enough to confront me to truly turn from my iniquities and give up my sins for God, and it was that idolatry and unrepentance which had been my downfall.

Just like Adam and Eve, Cain, Judas Iscariot, and many other people today, I believed IN God, but I had not understood the need to BELIEVE, TRUST, and OBEY God. Therefore, sin and death were still ruling in my life, and were still corrupting and destroying me.

Up to that point in life, yes, I was biologically and intellectually alive, but I was still spiritually dead because my sins were my idol. They took precedence in my life over God. I claimed to believe in God, but was still following Satan with my life, not God.

I understand now that God is a Spirit, and He created us as spiritual beings made in His own image and after His own likeness. Yet, before that day in my life, there was no spiritual relationship bond between myself and God because I had never let go of my intellect until that day.

While Satan was hounding me that day to commit suicide by turning my car into an oncoming truck, (in utter desperation) I reached out in FAITH to God with my spirit in complete submission to Him, admitting I had not been serving Him and crying out for help. When I finally did this, God heard my cry and came into my life personally, just as He has done with so many other people all around the world.

I went instantly from being spiritually dead to spiritually alive through the experience of having been born again by God's Spirit. Ever since then I have never had any doubt whatsoever that God is my Father in Heaven and what the Bible says about Jesus Christ is true, and that I am now part of God's family, His child. I know that God wants me to turn away from all evil and follow Christ because all Christians are being prepared in this life to become part of Christ's spiritual bride when He returns.

I am not saying that I have never stumbled in my Christian walk. Every Christian does. Every Christian is still vulnerable to sin's temptations because Satan is still our enemy who is looking to lead us astray with all of his lying tactics whenever we let our guard down.

Yet, those who truly know and love God do not WANT to keep sinning. We hate it when we fail God. Consequently we do not continue to practice sin daily. Rather, as Paul says, we learn to keep the evil that is part of our flesh under subjection to our reborn spirits which now want to believe, trust, and obey God.

Therefore I do not run like someone running aimlessly; I do not fight like a boxer beating the air. No, I strike a blow to my body and make it my slave so that after I have preached to others, I myself will not be disqualified for the prize. 1 Corinthians 9:26-27 NIV

It's not that God is keeping us under His iron hand, threatening us with losing our salvation if we sin. We just believe, trust and obey God now because we know God wants to keep us from the evil that has been consuming and destroying, not only us, but all others who are led astray by the deceitfulness of sin.

So, we ask the Holy Spirit to help us fight and overcome our sinful flesh and enable us to live a life that is pleasing to God. We believe God's Word when He tells us that there is now therefore no condemnation for those in Christ Jesus who do not walk according to the flesh, but live our lives according to the Holy Spirit who lives in us. We know that we can overcome every evil spirit because:

You are of God, little children, and have overcome them, because He who is in you is greater than he who is in the world. 1 John 4:4 NKJV

Can We Actually Know God and How Much He Really Loves Us?

There are certainly more than a few books already in print about the coming Rapture of the church, and yes, this book is also about the return of Jesus for His Bride and the "catching up" of believers in the Resurrection, plus a little bit about the 7 years of Tribulation which will follow the Rapture.

However, every author has their own reasons for writing their books, and I too have mine. After completing my first book **"Dangerous Journey Home"** (my own journey back to God through God's grace and faith in Jesus Christ) and my second book **"God is Light-Love-Life"** (a book to help people have a better grasp of what God is really like, and who Jesus really is), I spent close to a year seeking the guidance of the Holy Spirit to discern what the Lord would have me write about next.

In my own life, I never looked back from that day with God in 1981, and now with 40 years of Christian leadership and accumulated teaching, I knew I had more than enough information to write numerous other books to help bring new people to the Lord and hopefully guide those who are already Christians to come to a better understanding of God, the Holy Spirit and Jesus Christ.

Nonetheless, that does not mean that it is always easy for Christian authors to know what God would have us to write about next or how we may best serve the Lord with our writing. As I struggled with whether or not the world even needs another book about the Rapture and what I could say that would make my book any different from others that are already in print, I had a dream this morning, and in the dream I believe the Lord said to me:

"There are multitudes who know about Me, and yet they do not really KNOW Me or My character. Mankind in general has little understanding of how much I really love those whom I created, and how I am unwilling for any to perish, but desire that all should come to repentance and LIVE, not die. Tell them about Me. Tell them about My heart and My desires, and encourage them to come back to Me and live."

Does God still talk to people in dreams and visions? I believe He does. Over the years, I have experienced God's presence many times in many different ways since that first day when I gave my heart to Him on the floor of my car. I have even seen numerous miracles and healings during those many years of ministry.

If you have never experienced any of these things in your life, my advice is to stop spending so much time with unbelievers and start spending time in the company of men and women who have seen God move supernaturally, people of faith whose testimonies will encourage you to believe that God is the same today as he was 2000 years ago.

Yes, I believe God spoke to me this morning in a dream. Therefore, when you read this book about the soon-coming resurrection of those who love God, know that I have done my best to present it to you from the perspective of God being our loving Creator, our true Father in Heaven, with His Son being both our Bridegroom and our Savior.

I offer you this book to help you understand that God deeply desires us to be part of His eternal family with an unfathomable love that is so vast that we cannot even fully comprehend it. Yet, through our spirits, we can have faith to believe that every single thing God says in His Word is true.

Is Jesus coming to take us where He is? The truth is that one day soon, those who are followers of Christ will be caught up to be with God, and then we will know Jesus Christ as He already knows and loves us. Then, from that day forward, we shall be with Jesus forever and there will be no more doubt or questions in our minds about God or His plans, for we shall all know Him and be like Him.

Chapter 3

The Promise of the Bridegroom

The Great Falling Away

I know I keep repeating this, but it is important for us to remember that in a time period of less than 2,000 years, Christianity has grown from 12 Apostles and a little over 120 disciples at its inception, until now it has become the largest religion in the world, with well over 2 billion people professing to be followers of Jesus Christ.

God even said in the Scriptures that such explosive growth would occur until the gospel would be preached and become known in every nation of the world, but in the latter days, a great falling away would also occur, and finally, the end would come.

Yes, it's all coming true. From a humble beginning of a few people in one of the smallest countries in the world, Christianity has now become the largest religion on Earth, but much of the "Christianity" that is being preached today throughout the world is clearly not the same message to mankind that Jesus and the Apostles preached in the Bible.

In fact, ever since Jesus began preaching in Israel,

mankind has had difficulty believing what Jesus taught, and consequently, people keep trying to find God through the "tree of knowledge of good and evil". They keep taking other paths and trying to use human knowledge and intellect alone to find God, and it just doesn't work.

Shortly before Christ's death, the disciples all started to become deeply concerned when Jesus began to preach that He would soon be killed. They had thought Jesus would be taking over the world in His natural form, and they were concerned because (in all of human history) it was known that no human being had ever permanently come back from the dead.

Therefore, they had tremendous difficulty believing Christ's claim that He could rise from the dead after His crucifixion. So, Jesus took considerable time to comfort His followers and explain to them regarding His mission on Earth as a man. Jesus told them about coming to Earth from His Father in Heaven and His soon-coming death and departure. He told them He would be resurrected on the third day. He told them where He would be going, and that He would return to "catch up" those who believe on Him and take them WITH Him to where He now IS.

I came forth from the Father, and am come into the world: again, I leave the world, and go to the Father. John 16:28 NKJV

Let not your heart be troubled: ye believe in God, believe also in me. In my Father's house are many mansions: if it were not so, I would have told you. I go to prepare a place for you. And if I go and prepare a place for you, I will come again, and receive you unto myself; that where I am, there ye may be also. John 14:1-3 KJV

These declarations from Jesus are really not at all difficult for anyone to understand if we simply exercise faith to believe what Jesus said. Jesus said He came forth from God. He went back to Father God. He went there to prepare dwelling places for us. He will return to "receive" us unto Himself, so that where He NOW is, we shall be also.

The problem has never really been with mankind's ability to comprehend what Jesus said. It has always been about our willingness to BELIEVE what Jesus said. It is very important to note that Jesus did not tell His disciples (including us) that He would be arriving on Earth to be received by US, so that where we ARE, He will be also.

When Jesus returns to catch up His Bride, He will not at that time be coming to live on Earth where we now are. He won't even land on the Earth when He comes for us. Jesus said that WE will be caught up to be with HIM and we will be going to live for a time in Father God's House in Heaven where Jesus presently IS. That is why Jesus says to us: "I will come again and receive you unto myself; that where I am, you may be also."

After that, the Tribulation will begin and the wicked and unrepentant of humanity will learn what the horrors of seven years of life on Earth will be like under Satan's rule without God's hedge of protection to hinder evil.

We will not return to Earth until much later, when Armageddon (WWIII) and mankind's continued unrepentance is on the verge of destroying all life on Earth. Then, God says we will return to this world with Jesus to defeat Satan and all his followers. That is when we will take over rulership of the world as kings and priests ruling and reigning with Jesus.

Yet, God explains to us that (right from the beginning of Christianity) there were professing Christians preaching many different corrupted versions of what Jesus actually said. There were those who preached there was no resurrection and that Jesus was not raised. Some were saying that the resurrection had already occurred.

Still others were saying that Jesus had already returned, and lastly, there were also those who mocked the disciples' warnings for us to repent and remain in a constant state of faith and readiness for Christ's return to "catch us up" and take us with Him.

The Bride Will Go Where Jesus Is

This is the primary Biblical doctrine that many today are rejecting because they do not want to acknowledge the truth of Christ's warnings that the unrepentant (those continuing to practice iniquity) will NOT be going with Jesus when He arrives. Jesus said many will be left behind when He returns to redeem the bodies of all deceased believers and "catch up" all of Christ's living followers who are still alive when our Father in Heaven tells Jesus "Go and receive your Bride".

Many today do not want to believe that it will happen. They want to believe that everyone who CLAIMS to know Jesus will be going with Him when He comes. Or they want to believe that everything will continue just as it is and all professing Christians will have to go through the horrors of the entire seven year tribulation, of which the Bible tells us that almost none of the human race will survive:

Most importantly, I want to remind you that in the last days scoffers will come, mocking the truth and following their own desires. They will say, "What happened to the promise that Jesus is coming again? From before the times of our ancestors, everything has remained the same since the world was first created." 2 Peter 3:3-4 NLT

Later on, during the Apostle Paul's ministry, Paul took the time in 2 Thessalonians to warn people not to be deceived by all of this corrupt preaching and teaching. In connection with Paul's warnings, it is important to understand that in this next passage, Paul is addressing two separate topics, not one:

1. Paul made it clear that the day of Christ's return to set up His kingdom would not be happening until FIRST there would be a great falling away from the truth, and the Antichrist would come to power and invade Israel declaring himself to be God.

Now, brethren, concerning the coming of our Lord Jesus Christ and our gathering together to Him, we ask you, not to be soon shaken in mind or troubled, either by spirit or by word or by letter, as if from us, as though the day of Christ had come. Let no one deceive you by any means; for *that Day will not come* unless the falling away comes first, and the man of sin is revealed, the son of perdition, who opposes and exalts himself above all that is called God or that is worshiped, so that he sits as God in the temple of God, showing himself that he is God. 2 Thessalonians 2:1-4 NKJV

2. Those who think that the "Day" of the coming of the Lord to set up His kingdom, and our "gathering together to Him" (the Resurrection/Rapture) is referring to a single event are ignoring Paul's reminder to the Thessalonians and us in this passage that he already told Christians about our gathering together to Christ the last time he was in Thessalonica.

> Don't you remember that I told you about all this when I was with you? And you know what is holding him back, for he can be revealed only when his time comes. For this lawlessness is already at work secretly, and it will remain secret until the one who is holding it back steps out of the way. Then the man of lawlessness will be revealed, but the Lord Jesus will slay him with the breath of his mouth and destroy him by the splendor of his coming. 2 Thessalonians 2:5-8 NLT

So, the next questions are: When did Paul already tell them about this, and what did he say? Who is holding back the revelation of Antichrist? All we have to do is go back to Paul's first epistle to the Thessalonians to learn the answer. There Paul commends the Thessalonian church for turning back to serve the one true God. They were already suffering some persecution and affliction. Yet, Paul was still encouraging them to look for the return of Jesus to deliver those who are alive at Christ's return from the wrath that is to come upon the rest of the world:

> and to wait for His Son from heaven, whom He raised from the dead, *even* Jesus who delivers us from the wrath to come. 1 Thessalonians 1:10 NKJV

Paul had earlier written an epistle to the Corinthians re-affirming Christ's own resurrection and explaining how Jesus was the firstfruits of those who will be resurrected when Christ returns. Yes, Paul already said that those who are still alive at His arrival will be going to Heaven to be with Jesus. Now in 1 Corinthians and 1 Thessalonians, Paul goes on to encourage us by going into more detail about the coming resurrection and what has happened to the believers who are already deceased:

If in this life only we have hope in Christ, we are of all men most miserable. But now is Christ risen from the dead, and become the firstfruits of them that slept.

For since by man came death, by man came also the resurrection of the dead. For as in Adam all die, even so in Christ shall all be made alive. But every man in his own order: Christ the firstfruits; afterward they that are Christ's at his coming. 1 Corinthians 15:19-23 KJV

And now, dear brothers and sisters, we want you to know what will happen to the believers who have died so you will not grieve like people who have no hope. For since we believe that Jesus died and was raised to life again, we also believe that when Jesus returns, God will bring back with him the believers who have died. We tell you this directly from the Lord: We who are still living when the Lord returns will not meet him ahead of those who have died. For the Lord Himself will come down from heaven with a commanding shout, with the voice of the archangel, and with the trumpet call of God. First, the believers who have died will rise from their graves. Then, together with them, we who are still alive and remain on the earth will be caught up in the clouds to meet the Lord in the air. Then we will be with the Lord forever. So encourage each other with these words.

1 Thessalonians 4:13-18 NLT

Blessed be the God and Father of our Lord Jesus Christ, which according to his abundant mercy hath begotten us again unto a lively hope by the resurrection of Jesus Christ from the dead, to an inheritance incorruptible, and undefiled, and that fadeth not away, reserved in heaven for you 1 Peter 1:3-4 KJV

So, as a preacher, what are the words I should be using to encourage other believers as they see the planet around them collapsing ecologically and world society in the process of a headlong dive towards the beginning of the Tribulation that will end with WWIII (Armageddon) and the certain destruction of all flesh on Earth if Jesus does not return to put a stop to the insanity?

Should I tell people that Jesus is going to put His beloved Bride through all of this wrath for seven years to be "purified" or prove her worthiness? Or should I comfort the beloved of God by telling those who love Jesus that we are not appointed to endure God's wrath?

In spite of the reality that Christians have suffered tribulation and persecution since the time of the first Apostles, none of this is the wrath of God spoken of in Revelation, and I believe that God's Word reassures us that the coming Tribulation is not going to be God's seven year "torture test" for those who have been made righteous through faith in Jesus.

But fornication and all uncleanness or covetousness, let it not even be named among you, as is fitting for saints; neither filthiness, nor foolish talking, nor coarse jesting, which are not fitting, but rather giving of thanks. For this you know, that no fornicator, unclean person, nor covetous man, who is an idolater, has any inheritance in the kingdom of Christ and God. Let no one deceive you with empty words, for because of these things the wrath of God comes upon the sons of disobedience. Therefore do not be partakers with them. Ephesians 5:3-7 NKJV

Just as the law in the Old Testament was for the wicked, not the righteous, God reveals to us in His Word that the wrath of the seven year Tribulation will also be for the wicked, not the righteous.

Those last seven years will be the last opportunity God provides for the wicked to repent once they have experienced what life on Earth will be like without God's hedge of protection insulating mankind from the overspreading of evil that Satan is going to unleash upon Earth during his last seven years of rule over humanity.

Indeed, there WILL be multitudes who will repent, come to Jesus, and die saved during those seven years after the Rapture. It may even be the greatest single Christian revival in human history. God indicates that there will be a great multitude who will die for Christ during the Tribulation.

After these things I looked, and behold, a great multitude which no one could number, of all nations, tribes, peoples, and tongues, standing before the throne and before the Lamb, clothed with white robes, with palm branches in their hands, and crying out with a loud voice, saying, "Salvation *belongs* to our God who sits on the throne, and to the Lamb!" Revelation 7:9-10 NKJV

Then one of the elders answered, saying to me, "Who are these arrayed in white robes, and where did they come from?" And I said to him, "Sir, you know." So he said to me, "These are the ones who come out of the great tribulation, and washed their robes and made them white in the blood of the Lamb. Revelation 7:13-14 NKJV

Yet, still most of humanity will not repent and come to Jesus. We can know this because God Himself foretells the state of mankind at the end of the first half of the Tribulation:

But the people who did not die in these plagues still refused to repent of their evil deeds and turn to God. They continued to worship demons and idols made of gold, silver, bronze, stone, and wood—idols that can neither see nor hear nor walk! And they did not repent of their murders or their witchcraft or their sexual immorality or their thefts. Revelation 9:20-21 NLT

The above passage gives us the reason that God's wrath will keep coming to humanity during the second half of the Tribulation. In spite of all the evils that they have already seen and over half of mankind perishing, almost all of the remainder of humanity will still continue to refuse to repent and come to God.

What about us right now, today? Are we going to believe God's promise that there is an incorruptible inheritance reserved for us in Heaven? Or, are we going to keep following the Devil, always looking for another sign before we will depart from our wicked ways and turn to follow Jesus and be saved from His wrath?

Chapter 4

In the Beginning Mankind Was Safe

Safety in Believe, Trust, Obey

Did you know the Lord tells us in His Word that (even though God had His plan for man's salvation in place before the world was created), in the beginning, humanity did not need to be "saved"?

The book of Genesis tells us that when God created Adam and Eve, the Earth and the rest of the material universe, everything was created for man's dominion and inheritance, and it was all VERY GOOD. Mankind was completely "SAFE" with God. Adam and Eve even had the potential for eternal life as long as they continued to believe, trust and obey God.

In the beginning, Adam and Eve were spiritual beings just like we are. They were created by God in the image and likeness of God and placed within natural biological bodies for the purpose of reproducing after their own kind and they were completely safe from all evil. They had spiritual life, biological life and they had complete rule over everything on Earth. In fact, everything that God had created in the material universe (including humanity) was VERY GOOD

And God said, Let us make man in our image, after our likeness: and let them have dominion over the fish of the sea, and over the fowl of the air, and over the cattle, and over all the earth, and over every creeping thing that creepeth upon the earth. So God created man in his own image, in the image of God created he him; male and female created he them. And God blessed them, and God said unto them, Be fruitful, and multiply, and replenish the earth, and subdue it: and have dominion over the fish of the sea, and over the fowl of the air, and over every living thing that moveth upon the earth. Genesis 1:26-28 KJV

And God saw everything that he had made, and, behold, it was very good. And the evening and the morning were the sixth day. Genesis 1:31 KJV

God even tells us that (in the beginning) Adam and Eve had the potential for ETERNAL life through eating from the Tree of Life. The Book of Revelation reveals to us that the Tree of Life was a very special tree bearing a different manner of fruit every month, plus the purpose of the leaves from the Tree of Life was that they could be applied for healing of any accidental injury to man's natural biological bodies.

The LORD God made all sorts of trees grow up from the ground—trees that were beautiful and that produced delicious fruit. In the middle of the garden he placed the tree of life and the tree of the knowledge of good and evil. Genesis 2:9 NLT

Then the angel showed me a river with the water of life, clear as crystal, flowing from the throne of God and of the Lamb. It flowed down the center of the main street. On each side of the river grew a tree of life, bearing twelve crops of fruit, with a fresh crop each month. The leaves were used for medicine to heal the nations. Revelation 22:1-2 NLT

So, in the beginning, mankind was completely safe from death and all manner of external evil. Even accidental injury to their natural biological bodies could be healed by applying the leaves from the tree of life.

Yes, there was also a tree of knowledge of good and evil growing right in the middle of the Garden of Eden alongside the Tree of Life, but Adam and Eve were still "safe" in God from evil in the beginning. All they had to do was to heed God's command never to eat from the tree of knowledge of good and evil. All they had to do to stay safe in God forever was to continue to BELIEVE, TRUST and OBEY God.

God also warned them that if they did choose to eat from that tree (which would signal their desire and decision to "know" both good AND evil) they would surely die. It is very, very important to note here that God did not say that HE would kill them, only that they would die (or more accurately, begin to die) from the day that they ate from that tree.

The Lord God placed the man in the Garden of Eden to tend and watch over it. But the Lord God warned him, "You may freely eat the fruit of every tree in the garden except the tree of the knowledge of good and evil. If you eat its fruit, you are sure to die." Genesis 2:15-17 NLT

The Fall of Mankind

In Genesis we have the truth. In the beginning mankind obviously believed IN God because Adam and Eve knew God. They walked and talked with God and were completely safe from evil in God's family as long as they continued to BELIEVE, TRUST, and OBEY God. Safety comes from believing, trusting, and obeying God.

Then along came Satan, concealing his presence within the body of the serpent like the deceiver and coward that he is. So, what is the first thing Satan does? He LIES to Eve (and to Adam - who is right there listening with her). And what was Satan's deceptive message?

1. Don't believe God. You won't die.

2. Don't trust God. God is keeping this knowledge of evil from you because He knows you'll become wise, like gods if you eat from this tree.

3. Don't obey God. Reject His fatherhood. Believe me. Trust me. Obey me.

What does God's Word say about what happened next? It says that when Adam and Eve rejected God, their hearts were **darkened**. Darkness came into their being and they became fools.

For the invisible things of him from the creation of the world are clearly seen, being understood by the things that are made, even his eternal power and Godhead; so that they are without excuse: Because that, when they knew God, they glorified him not as God, neither were thankful; but became vain in their imaginations, and their foolish heart was darkened. Professing themselves to be wise, they became fools, Romans 1:20-22 KJV

Who changed the truth of God into a lie, and worshipped and served the creature more than the Creator, who is blessed forever. Amen. Romans 1:25 KJV

If Satan had been an honest being, rather than the father of all lies, instead of telling Adam and Eve that they would continue to live, and adding the knowledge of evil would make them wise like gods, he would perhaps have told them this:

Until now, everything you have known or will ever know is "very good". But if you choose to embrace the knowledge of good AND evil, I will bring a curse and corruption to everything in your domain. Even the Earth will groan under the curse of evil that I will bring into your existence. Nature itself will rebel against you with weeds and thorns and thistles and predatory animals. Your perfect natural biological bodies that God has given you will become corrupted and begin to deteriorate with sickness and decay until eventually they will no longer be able to function anymore and then they will die. But even then you will continue to be subject to me and remain under my evil dominion after you die, for your spirits will remain imprisoned under my control forever, first in hell, and then in the Lake of Fire.

Maybe if Satan had said THAT to Eve, she might have thought twice before eating from the tree. Yet we all know the outcome of man's first encounter with Satan. Both Eve (and her husband, Adam, who was with her) ate from the forbidden tree. The knowledge of evil became part of human nature, and here we are.

Of course, in spite of Adam and Eve's foolish decision, God is a loving and merciful God who did not want his own offspring to remain corrupted by evil and continue to be tormented under Satan's rule for all eternity. Therefore, God in His mercy already had a plan in place for mankind's redemption and restoration back into God's family again.

God made a promise to Adam and Eve that one day a REDEEMER would be born from Eve's offspring and this Redeemer would crush Satan and his hold over mankind forever.

Then God evicted Adam and Eve from the Garden of Eden (where the Tree of Life was) so that they would not also eat from that tree and be condemned to continue to live for all eternity with evil. God did not do this as punishment, but because the Lord did not want evil corrupting their being forever until it consumed all the good that was in them. God did not want them to become like Satan is today, totally evil, with no good left in him.

Adam and Eve Lost their Covering

There was also another consequence to Adam and Eve's sin that most people are not aware of because it is rarely taught. Many people do not know that Adam and Eve were originally "clothed" or infused with the glory of God, which was the result of abiding in God's presence in their perfect sinless state.

In the beginning, God's Holy Spirit permeated their entire being and shone out from within them with tremendous brilliance as their clothing or covering. They were never without light because the glory of God burst forth from their very being as the result of walking and talking with God in their sinless state. Wherever Adam and Eve went, all of creation knew that THIS was the son and daughter of God because God's glory shone from them continuously.

If you have never heard of this before (or if you doubt what I am saying) let me take you on a journey through the Word of God to explain it to you. In the beginning, Adam and Eve's whole being was "very good". There was nothing within them to prevent them from walking and talking with God in God's glorified presence. As a result of this, God's glory shone forth from them even more brightly than it did from Moses when he came back down to Israel from being in God's presence.

How do we know that this is true? If you don't know the story of Moses and his meetings with God, this is how it goes. God originally communicated with Moses alone on the mountain in the vicinity of a bush which was burning, but was not consumed.

Then, after God delivered Israel from Egypt, Moses went up Mt. Sinai to speak with God again, and Moses asks to see God. However, God told Moses that in man's corrupted spiritual state, his body would not be able to tolerate all of God's goodness without being destroyed, and Moses would die.

No one in our present sinful state can see God and

continue to live a mortal life because our corrupted natural bodies would be destroyed. So God told Moses to go into a rock cleft and the Lord covered him with his hand until He had passed by. (See Exodus 33:18-23).

Moses was only permitted to see God's back as God's presence passed by and was receding, and this was enough to "infuse" the body of Moses with so much glory that when he came down from the mountain, the exposed flesh of his face emanated so much light for days that Israel was actually afraid to look at him. Moses had to physically cover his face with a veil to dim the light that was being emitted from his body or nobody would come near him.

Now it was so, when Moses came down from Mount Sinai (and the two tablets of the Testimony *were* in Moses' hand when he came down from the mountain), that Moses did not know that the skin of his face shone while he talked with Him. So when Aaron and all the children of Israel saw Moses, behold, the skin of his face shone, and they were afraid to come near him. EXODUS 34:29-30 NKJV

The old way, with laws etched in stone, led to death, though it began with such glory that the people of Israel could not bear to look at Moses' face. For his face shone with the glory of God, even though the brightness was already fading away. 2 Corinthians 3:7 NLT

Whenever Moses went up the mountain, or later on when Moses was exposed to God's presence in the Ark, the body of Moses exuded this wonderful glory for a while after being in God's partial presence. However, Moses was not without sin, so God warned him that his corrupted natural body would not be able to tolerate the full glory of God. Furthermore, Moses found that even the glory that he did absorb would fade over time, like water leaking from a flawed container, and Moses would have to go back into God's presence again for a "recharge."

Yet that was not the case with Adam and Eve in the beginning and neither was it the case with Jesus on the mountain of transfiguration. For a short time, Christ allowed his disciples to see the full glory of God shining forth from His sinless natural body the same way it would have been able to shine forth from Adam and Eve in the presence of God in the beginning, before they chose to embrace evil.

In contrast to Moses, the glory that would have shone forth from Adam and Eve in their sinless state would have been much greater than that of Moses, similar to that which Jesus demonstrated when He spoke with Moses and Elijah on the mountain and was transfigured before His disciples:

Six days later Jesus took Peter and the two brothers, James and John, and led them up a high mountain to be alone. ² As the men watched, Jesus' appearance was transformed so that his face shone like the sun, and his clothes became as white as light. Matthew 17:1-2 NLT

This was not Jesus revealing His Deity as many have supposed. This was Jesus showing us what sinless human beings in a natural uncorrupted body really look like when they are "clothed" with the glory of God shining forth from them.

Many people do not understand (or have never been

taught) that when the New Jerusalem comes down from Heaven, the reason there will be no need of the sun, moon and stars for light, and the reason that there will be no darkness at all anymore is that the glory of God will be shining forth from Jesus and the resurrected/raptured believers.

This glorious light of the Holy Spirit exuding from within every sinless believer will illuminate the new Earth and be our light wherever we go, and God says that this light will be so bright that there will be no longer be any **darkness** anywhere. When the Heavenly Jerusalem comes down from the Third Heaven to become Earth's eternal capital city, Jesus and His Bride will be its light.

And the city has no need of sun or moon, for the glory of God illuminates the city, and the Lamb is its light. The nations will walk in its light, and the kings of the world will enter the city in all their glory. Its gates will never be closed at the end of day because there is no night there. And all the nations will bring their glory and honor into the city. Revelation 21:23-26 NLT

No longer will there be a curse upon anything. For the throne of God and of the Lamb will be there, and his servants will worship him. And they will see his face, and his name will be written on their foreheads. And there will be no night there—no need for lamps or sun—for the Lord God will shine on them. And they will reign forever and ever. Revelation 22:3-5 NLT

The Knowledge of Good and Evil

There are numerous preachers today who mistakenly teach that Adam and Eve choosing to know evil was all part of God's desired plan, that it all had to happen in order for humanity to "know" the difference between good and evil, and to comprehend the fullness of God's love and goodness.

Their explanations might sound reasonable to some, but they are not at all Biblical. The suggestion that one cannot fully know what goodness is without first knowing evil is simply untrue. It is not an accurate representation of what God is like, or the future that God wanted for humanity.

First of all, to say that Adam and Eve HAD to learn evil removes the responsibility and guilt from Adam and Eve for disobeying God and places the blame on God for evil's presence in the world.

Furthermore, this kind of teaching totally ignores the fact that in His thirty-three year natural life span, Jesus Christ had no problem in fully discerning the presence of evil and comprehending what evil is without ever allowing evil to become part of His nature. THAT is the kind of life that God wanted for Adam and Eve, but they chose to trust and obey the Devil instead.

The life of Jesus Christ is living proof to us that Adam and Eve never had to embrace evil and make it part of their nature as human beings in order to discern what evil was and avoid it. They had the goodness of God within them to be able to comprehend evil without ever participating in evil.

The life of Jesus demonstrates to us that, even though evil showed up in the Garden of Eden (in the form of Satan concealed within the body of the serpent) it was possible for Adam and Eve to spiritually discern and understand what evil is. They could have avoided evil by believing, trusting and obeying God without ever actually embracing and practicing it.

How did Jesus remain sinless when there was evil all around Him during His life on Earth? The reason Jesus was able to do this is that there are actually two kinds of knowledge. The first is knowledge of all that is "very good". This is a spiritual and comprehensive knowledge which comes to us through BELIEVING, TRUSTING and OBEYING God.

This knowledge includes the capacity to "discern" between good and evil through faith in God and guidance from the Holy Spirit, without ever having to experience or participate in evil itself.

It is important to grasp that (although Adam and Eve were created innocent of evil) they were not created primitive, stupid, or mentally deficient in any way. They were not created incapable of discerning or comprehending what evil is or how to avoid it.

The tree of knowledge of good and evil was not a tree whose purpose was to give Adam and Eve the ability to DISCERN or comprehend evil. They already had that ability through belief, trust, and obedience to God and His goodness. The tree of knowledge of good AND evil represented adding the kind of knowledge known as EXPERIENTIAL knowledge.

Adam and Eve already had the comprehensive or intellectual knowledge of "very good", and as long as they continued to believe, trust, and obey God, the only experiences they would ever have had for eternity would have all have been "very good".

However, man was not created as a mindless robot with no free will. The presence of the tree of knowledge of good and evil in the garden gave man the freedom (against God's wishes) to add the EXPERIENTIAL knowledge of knowing evil through allowing evil to occur within and become part of their being and domain.

Let me offer a simplified illustration of what I am talking about, using our own children as an example. When I grew up, we had a wood stove in the middle of the kitchen that was used for both cooking and heating, plus an oil furnace in the living room of the home when we needed more heat during the winter. These things were dangerous to touch when hot, and every good parent in the world of that generation would warn their children not to touch the stove when it was hot. Yet I think you know where this is heading.

When I was young, we were warned never to touch the stove when it was on. We were not even allowed to play near the stove because our parents knew that even if we accidentally touched the stove through carelessness, it was still capable of causing us terrible pain, injury, and possible permanent scarring through burning our skin, and they did not want any of that to happen to us.

Therefore (through FAITH in what our parents told us) as long as we believed our parents, every child in the world of my generation already had the intellectual or comprehensive knowledge that the stoves were hot and would injure us. We already HAD that comprehensive knowledge without ever actually having to experience the pain and injury that would be the result of disobeying our parents and touching the stove.

Yes, we all had the ability to intellectually know or discern that the stove was hot and would hurt us through

FAITH in what our parents had told us. Yet, I don't think I ever knew any child (including myself) who had never been burned, either by carelessness or deliberate experimentation as a result of touching one of those hot stoves.

After experiencing the painful consequences of disobedience or carelessness, we then finally learned to believe, trust, and obey what our parents had already told us, because we then understood by the pain of EXPERIENTIAL knowledge what they were trying to protect us from, and we then knew from experience that what they had told us was true. Yet, our parents never wanted any of us have the pain of that experiential knowledge, and neither does God.

The truth is that God has never desired that mankind would ever know evil by EXPERIENCE. That is why He created Adam and Eve in the beginning with the intellect to be able to discern between good and evil. Yes, God created mankind with the freedom to obey or reject His love, but the Lord has always had the desire that mankind would experientially only know goodness and blessing.

When Adam and Eve ate from the tree, it was in response to Satan's temptation to man to gain knowledge about evil through EXPERIENCING and participating in evil.

It was Satan's goal from the very beginning to try to turn humanity against God and make evil part of their nature against God's wishes, knowing that over time evil would consume and corrupt all that is good within mankind because it is the very nature of evil to do so. Satan almost succeeded. Evil almost eradicated humanity in Noah's day, and now here we are again in these end times almost at the very same place, suggesting that man has learned very little about God in six thousand years.

Man's First Tries at False Religion

What happened to Adam and Eve when they chose to embrace the knowledge of evil? God explains to us in the Scriptures what happened. God has declared to us that evil shall not dwell with Him.

For thou art not a God that hath pleasure in wickedness: neither shall evil dwell with thee. Psalm 5:4 KJV

Therefore, in order for the darkness of evil to come into Adam and Eve's being, God's presence, His light, their "covering" of God's glory had to leave. As we already read in Romans 1, when Adam and Eve rejected God and chose to obey Satan's urging to embrace evil, their foolish hearts were **"darkened"**. The glory of God had to depart to make room for the darkness.

When that happened, it became painfully obvious to Adam and Eve that they were naked. The glory that was their covering was gone, and for the first time in their lives, they experienced the fear and shame that is part of evil. It was this fear and shame which led to man's first attempt at false religion. Adam and Eve tried to cover their nakedness with leaves and they tried to conceal their sin from God by physically hiding from the Lord when He showed up in the Garden.

God soon made it clear to Adam and Eve that their own efforts to hide their sin or cover their nakedness using a false fig leaf religion was not going to be adequate to please God and bring them back into relationship with Him. Adam and

Eve would have to REPENT.

They would have to turn away from evil, away from their own religion, their own attempt at righteousness. They would have to listen to God's instructions and obediently follow what God told them to do if they wanted their sin to be covered until God's promised Redeemer came to free them from Satan's dominion so they could be allowed back into God's family again.

What was God's requirement? What was God's original covenant with Adam and Eve? The Lord took away Adam and Eve's bloodless covering of leaves and made clothing for them from the skins of some of the first animals on Earth to die.

Some have suggested that God slew the animals, but the Scriptures do not elaborate on that. I think it is more likely that (since God is a God of life and Satan is the one who holds the power of death) as soon as Adam and Eve surrendered their dominion to him, Satan started causing some animals to fall dead right in front of Adam and Eve, and God took the skins from some of these animals to cover their nakedness.

Unto Adam also and to his wife did the Lord God make coats of skins, and clothed them. Genesis 3:21 KJV

From that time forward, as a sign that man was repentant and desired to believe and return to God, Adam and Eve understood that they and their descendants were to make their clothing from the skins of dead animals, to cover themselves.

This would be a constant reminder that it was humanity's desire to embrace the knowledge of evil that had brought sin and death into mankind's domain. Adam and Eve did not know it at the time, but it was also a prophetic prelude, a "shadow" of what Jesus Christ would later do for mankind. He would allow His own blood to be shed for humanity, and His blood would not just cover man's sins. Christ's death would cancel them, making us acceptable to God again.

However, it would not have taken Adam and Eve very long to find that if there was no fresh carcass available when new clothes were needed, Adam would then have to go through the agonizing experience of having to slay an animal himself to make their clothing. This would have been necessary because, once dead, animals who die naturally soon began to stink and rot away as they are eaten with worms and insects.

Yet, just as important as the clothing God required them to wear, Adam and Eve understood that to please the Lord, God expected them to continue to REPENT or "turn away" from following Satan and walk with God again, and they were to teach their children to do the same. The common factor of all of the early heroes of the Bible is that they "walked with God", not Satan.

Adam and Eve actually got off to a good start in their desire to return to God. Unlike many of the women of our generation (who falsely believe that their unborn children are only part of their body tissue and therefore their own property to either nourish or kill) Eve understood that the first child growing in her womb was actually created by GOD and a gift from God.

Eve realized that this was not her child alone. She grasped that her son was God's offspring whom she would be taking care of. She understood that man and woman's sexual union only provide the sperm and the egg that will unite to make our natural biological body.

It is God who gives that body life, and it is God who knits the being whom He has created to that natural body, forming us in our mother's wombs. Really, all the human parents do is just provide the biological "house" which enables God's newly created child to live and function in while we are in this material world.

And Adam knew Eve his wife; and she conceived, and bare Cain, and said, I have gotten a man from the Lord. Genesis 4:1 KJV

You made all the delicate, inner parts of my body and knit me together in my mother's womb. Thank you for making me so wonderfully complex! Your workmanship is marvelous—how well I know it. You watched me as I was being formed in utter seclusion, as I was woven together in the dark of the womb. You saw me before I was born. Psalm 139:13-16 NLT

Speaking of our natural bodies and our resurrected/raptured bodies, God had this to say through the inspired writings of the Apostle Paul.

For we know that if our earthly house, *this* tent, is destroyed, we have a building from God, a house not made with hands, eternal in the heavens. For in this we groan, earnestly desiring to be clothed with our habitation which is from heaven, if indeed, having been clothed, we shall not be found naked. For we who are in *this* tent groan, being burdened, not because we want to be unclothed, but further clothed, that mortality may be swallowed up by life.

2 Corinthians 5:1-4 NKJV

Yes, I know that there are some who say the reason that Eve's first son Cain was evil was that he was the product of a sexual union between Eve and Satan, but that is an invention of their own evil imaginations. There is nothing at all in the Bible which says such a thing.

Rather, during the conversation between God and Cain later on in Genesis, we see God's love and concern for Cain as His son and God's desire for Cain to choose the right path to travel in life so that Cain might be restored to God's family again.

Then, in Genesis 4:2 and following, God tells us that Adam and Eve had a second child, whom they named Abel. God explains that Cain became a farmer to provide food for the family like his father Adam, but Abel chose to be a keeper of the sheep which, among other uses, would help to provide clothing for the family.

God then goes on to state that after a passage of time, both Cain and Abel voluntarily perform a religious deed, an act of worship to God. They both give a free-will offering to God from the work of their hands, and God accepts Abel's offering, but rejects Cain's. So, the question then becomes, "Why did God accept Abel's sacrifice and reject Cain's?"

I have heard numerous sermons on this topic, where preachers suggest that the reason God accepted Abel's offering and rejected Cain's was that Cain was not giving God the best of his crop, but there is nothing in the Scriptures to actually suggest that this is true.

Others have said that it was because Abel's sacrifice was a "blood" sacrifice, showing that he acknowledged that the shedding of blood was necessary to cover his sins, while Cain's offering was bloodless. However, God at this time in history was not REQUIRING any blood sacrifices for voluntary offerings of worship. God was only requiring that man's clothes be made from animal skins.

Neither is there any indication anywhere in the Scriptures that there was anything at all wrong with the content of Cain's offering, or in his choice of vocation to become a farmer like his father, Adam, instead of a shepherd. Both men had honorable professions.

In order to really understand what was going on with Cain and Abel, and learn why God rejected Cain, we have to compare the story in Genesis with what God says about sacrifices and about Cain and Abel elsewhere in the Bible.

This is an example of why it is so important to study the whole Bible and not just listen to preachers if we want to have a better understanding of God and our relationship with God. I think that a good place to start in helping our understanding of Cain and Abel is recorded in the Book of Psalms.

The sacrifice you desire is a broken spirit. You will not reject a broken and repentant heart, O God. Psalm 51:17 NLT

The Lord *is* near to those who have a broken heart, And saves such as have a contrite spirit. Psalm 34:18 NKJV

From here we see that God is not so much impressed by the content of our sacrifice as He is by the state of the heart of the person making the sacrifice. Then, if we go elsewhere in the Bible, we find that there was a very notable difference between the state of Abel's spirit and heart, and that of his brother, Cain.

In Hebrews 11, God testifies that Abel was a man of FAITH and that it was Abel's faith in God that made him righteous and made his sacrifice more excellent than Cain's. In fact, when Jesus was talking about God's prophets, He actually includes Abel as the first of the prophets.

This mention of Abel as a prophet suggests that Abel was not only a man who lived righteously, but he preached faith and righteousness to others as well (because that is what prophets do). With his prophetic anointing, it is very probable that it was Abel's preaching and encouraging Cain to turn from his wicked ways and come back to God that was the reason he was killed by his brother. It is a pattern that has repeated itself over and over all throughout human history.

By faith Abel offered to God a more excellent sacrifice than Cain, through which he obtained witness that he was righteous... Hebrews 11:4 NKJV

Therefore the wisdom of God also said, 'I will send them prophets and apostles, and *some* of them they will kill and persecute,' that the blood of all the prophets which was shed from the foundation of the world may be required of this generation, from the blood of Abel to the blood of Zechariah who perished between the altar and the temple. Yes, I say to you, it shall be required of this generation. Luke 11:49-51 NKJV

What about Cain? What was there about Cain and his life that caused God to reject his offering? There was actually a serious problem in Cain's life that God wanted to deal with because God loved Cain. We see in Genesis 4 that Cain became angry and depressed and his face showed his dejection after God rejected his gift. So God talked to Cain about the problem:

"Why are you so angry?" the Lord asked Cain. "Why do you look so dejected? You will be accepted if you do what is right. But if you refuse to do what is right, then watch out! Sin is crouching at the door, eager to control you. But you must subdue it and be its master." Genesis 4:6-7 NLT

What did God mean when He said to Cain "You will be accepted if you do what is right, but if you refuse to do what is right, watch out, sin is crouching at the door, eager to control you"? God was not talking about there being something wrong with the content of Cain's offering as some have suggested. God was talking about THE WAY CAIN WAS LIVING HIS LIFE, as explained in John's epistle:

We must not be like Cain, who belonged to the evil one and killed his brother. And why did he kill him? Because Cain had been doing what was evil, and his brother had been doing what was righteous. 1 John 3:12 NLT

What then can we learn from the story of Adam, Eve, and Cain? We can learn that even if we know God, talk with God, and spend time with Him, our evil behavior will still separate us from God, and continuing in evil behavior will make our religion and sacrifices unacceptable to God.

God requires more of us than just believing He exists and just believing that Jesus is the Son of God if we want to be saved. Even the devils believe that much, but they will never be saved because they refuse to depart from evil.

The problem with most of humanity is that the wicked refuse to REPENT of their wicked ways, and many professing Christians today are making the exact same mistake that Cain made by thinking that they can call Jesus their Savior while they continue to follow devils with their evil behavior. This is NOT acceptable to God. Nor can we be saved if we continue in this way.

Even in the New Testament, God tells us of Judas Iscariot, a man who was personally chosen by Jesus to be one of His twelve disciples. Judas walked and talked with Jesus. He gave to the poor from the money he was entrusted with. He was even anointed by Jesus to lay hands on the sick to heal them and to cast out devils, and yet the Scriptures tell us that he was an unrepentant man.

Judas remained a thief throughout his entire time with Jesus, stealing from the funds that were entrusted to him for the poor, and even criticizing Mary when she washed the feet of Jesus with a very expensive ointment because his desire was to steal the ointment and sell it for his own profit:

But Judas Iscariot, the disciple who would soon betray him, said, "That perfume was worth a year's wages. It should have been sold and the money given to the poor." Not that he cared for the poor—he was a thief, and since he was in charge of the disciples' money, he often stole some for himself. John 12:4-6 NLT

Later on, in Matthew 26, after a similar complaint by his disciples, initiated again (no doubt) by Judas for the same reason, Jesus rebukes them a second time. From the context, it appears that Judas was offended by this second rebuke from Jesus, for he immediately went out to the Jews and asked them how much they will pay him to betray Jesus:

> Then one of the twelve, called Judas Iscariot, went unto the chief priests, And said unto them, What will ye give me, and I will deliver him unto you? And they covenanted with him for thirty pieces of silver. And from that time he sought opportunity to betray him. Matthew 26: 14-16 KJV

Even then, it was still not too late for Judas. The last opportunity for Judas to repent of his idolatry of money would happen just two days later when Jesus announced to His twelve disciples during the Passover meal that He knew one of them would betray Him. But still Judas would not confess that he was the one who was planning to betray Jesus for money and repent of his sin.

When Jesus indicated to Judas that He knew it was him, Judas still would not repent, and his refusal to do so opened the door for him to be possessed by Satan himself who then led Judas out to betray Jesus for money. From the life of Judas, we can see how it is the nature of evil to become ever more destructive in our lives. The thievery of Judas probably started out with a little pilfering here and there from the offerings, but eventually degenerated into such an obsession with money that (for a few silver coins) Judas betrayed the only one who ever really loved him. Then later on, Satan oppressed the man so greatly that Judas killed himself in utter despair.

God's testimony in Scripture of Adam and Eve, Cain,

Judas Iscariot, and many other Biblical figures should be a loud warning to all of us that God requires more from the human race than just a willingness to believe that there is a God and that Jesus Christ is the Son of God and man's Savior. During His ministry, even Jesus Himself pondered the question:

...when the Son of Man returns, how many will he find on the earth who have faith?" Luke 18:8 NLT

When we look at the general state of the modern church in these end times, sometimes I wonder how much we have really learned of the lessons that God is trying to teach us. Yet, if we learn to listen to and follow the Holy Spirit, whom God has given us, we CAN learn to believe, trust, and obey God. That way, when Jesus does come for His Bride, we will be recognized by Christ as both faithful servants and Christ's beloved Bride who will be caught up to His Father's House to be with Him.

Chapter 5

How Can We Please God?

Believe-Trust-Obey

How then shall we please God in these end times? Please don't lose patience with me. I have a very good reason for going over all these other things before proceeding to the reason this book was primarily written, which is to teach people about the soon coming return of Jesus Christ for His Bride, His body (the church).

Everybody wants to know exactly when Jesus will be returning and every professing Christian thinks (or at least hopes) that he or she will be among those going with Jesus whenever He does come, but the giant elephants in the room, those that nobody wants to talk about, are God's repeated warnings to us in His Word:

Not everyone who says to me, 'Lord, Lord,' will enter the kingdom of heaven, but only the one who does the will of my Father who is in heaven. Many will say to me on that day, 'Lord, Lord, did we not prophesy in your name and in your name drive out demons and in your name perform many miracles?' Then I will tell them plainly, 'I never knew you. Away from me, you evildoers!' Matthew 7:21-23 NIV

Enter through the narrow gate. For wide is the gate and broad is the road that leads to destruction, and many enter through it. But small is the gate and narrow the road that leads to life, and only a few find it. Matthew 7:13-14 NIV

When you follow the desires of your sinful nature, the results are very clear: sexual immorality, impurity, lustful pleasures, idolatry, sorcery, hostility, quarreling, jealousy, outbursts of anger, selfish ambition, dissension, division, envy, drunkenness, wild parties, and other sins like these. Let me tell you again, as I have before, that anyone living that sort of life will not inherit the Kingdom of God. Galatians 5:19-21 NLT

When we study these Scriptures and many more like them, I would venture to say that the most important thing for us to know is not exactly WHEN Jesus will return, but how we can be pleasing to God with our lives NOW, today, because it will be those who are pleasing to God and walking with God who will be going with Him when He comes for His Bride. All who do NOT please God are going be left behind with the rest of the evildoers, regardless of whether or not they claim to be Christians and know God.

The truth is that we CAN know the answer to the questions that are important to our salvation. God's unchanging message goes all the way back to the Garden of Eden and it still applies today, because God is the same yesterday, today, and forever. As stated earlier in this book, in the beginning,

Adam and Eve did not need to be "saved" when they were first created. They were completely SAFE in God as long as they continued to believe, trust and obey the Lord.

Then along came Satan, and what was his lie? He told them they did not need to believe, trust, and obey God. Satan told Adam and Eve that they could obey him (the Devil) instead of God, and life would be even better for them. Satan even promised them they would become like (evolve into) gods if they believed and followed him. Yet the Devil's lies did not produce the promised results in Adam and Eve's life. Rejection of God only brought them evil, sorrow, sickness, pain and death.

The same lies did not work in Cain's life. They did not work for the entire human population in Noah's day. They did not work at the tower of Babel, or at Sodom and Gomorrah, and they did not work for the nation of Israel.

When Israel disobeyed God and chose to follow Satan, they went into bondage to other nations for centuries until God sent Moses to deliver them.

Neither did it work for Israel later when they claimed to be children of God, Abraham, and disciples of Moses, but rejected Jesus. The nation of Israel had their branch broken off from God's family tree and God grafted in the spiritual "nation" of the church of Jesus Christ into His family as man's avenue of salvation.

Then Jesus asked them, "Didn't you ever read this in the Scriptures? 'The stone that the builders rejected has now become the cornerstone. This is the Lord's doing, and it is wonderful to see.' I tell you, the Kingdom of God will be taken away from you and given to a nation that will produce the proper fruit. Matthew 21:43-43 NLT

But you are not like that, for you are a chosen people. You are royal priests, a **holy nation,** God's very own possession. As a result, you can show others the goodness of God, for he called you out of the darkness into his wonderful light. 1 Per 2:9 NLT

It did not work for Judas Iscariot as a disciple of Jesus, and as we have just read in Galatians 5, and now in 1 Corinthians 6, continuing in wickedness will not work today either for any people who claim to be Christians and say they know Jesus, but still reject God and continue to serve Satan with their behavior:

Know ye not that the unrighteous shall not inherit the kingdom of God? Be not deceived: neither fornicators, nor idolaters, nor adulterers, nor effeminate, nor abusers of themselves with mankind, Nor thieves, nor covetous, nor drunkards, nor revilers, nor extortioners, shall inherit the kingdom of God. 1 Corinthians 6:9-10 KJV

Yes, Paul points out in the Word of God that some true Christians WERE ONCE like that, but we do not live our lives like that anymore because we have now been washed, sanctified and justified by Jesus through the power of the Holy Spirit:

And such were some of you: but ye are washed, but ye are sanctified, but ye are justified in the name of the Lord Jesus, and by the Spirit of our God. 1 Corinthians 6:11 KJV

Yet, here we are six thousand years later, and, as illogical as it seems, many professing Christians in these end times are still believing, trusting, and following the same old lies that Satan successfully used on Adam and Eve in the Garden of Eden, and even a few more.

Yes, some modern preachers have added further deceptions to Satan's original bag of lies, including an attempt to redefine (lie about) what John the Baptist, AND Jesus, AND Peter, AND Paul, AND the Holy Spirit really mean when they command us to "REPENT" for the kingdom of heaven is at hand if we want to go with Jesus when He returns for His Bride.

Grace- Faith-Repentance-Works

The three main deceptive slogans that are being repeatedly promoted by those who are leading many people astray in these end times are:

1. "Repent" as it is used in the Bible always means nothing more than "change your mind" about believing in Jesus. They claim that repentance has nothing to do with human behavior.

2. God's Covenant with mankind regarding salvation is unconditional, so salvation can never be forfeited.

3. "Repentance" and "Works" are the same thing.

Since two of these errors are directly connected to repentance, let's begin by dealing with the Biblical definition of "repentance" as it relates to salvation. While it is perfectly true to say that the word (or a version of the word) "repent" can sometimes mean "regret" or a "change of thinking" as it is used in the Bible, this only a small part of what "repentance" means when God uses the word in the Bible in context to salvation.

We must remember that (just the same as with a huge abundance of other English words) the word "repent" has numerous meanings, and the accurate meaning of "REPENT" when it is used in the Bible depends on the Scriptural context in which it is used.

This also brings us to the common confusion among many Christians about what it means to be "saved by grace and not of works, lest any man should boast". There are many professing Christians today who are clearly unrepentant while they wave the banners of "I am saved by grace through faith and not of works" and "Don't judge people!"

Unfortunately, the reason that many people use these phrases is two-fold. First it is because many have been falsely taught that repentance and obedience are the same thing as "works". Second, it is because many professing Christians want to keep sinning and they want other Christians and Christian leaders to shut up and not talk to them about it.

Therefore, whenever you try to talk to these people about repentance and obedience, all they hear is "works" because, either they do not know the Scriptures, or they WANT to believe that repentance, obedience and works are all the same thing because they do not want to depart from continuing to work iniquity.

So, on one hand, we have professing Christians being led astray by those who try to suggest that (with regards to salvation) "repentance" means nothing more than "changing your mind" about whether or not you believe in Jesus. Then, there are just as many others who have incorrectly been taught that repentance and obedience are the same thing as works, and they know that the Bible says that good works alone can't save us. Therefore they have mistakenly gotten it into their thinking that God does not require repentance for salvation.

Yet, none of those teachings are Biblical. They are all trees bearing bad fruit, and many people's lives are being corrupted and destroyed all over the world in these end times because they think they can claim to be Christian, still follow the Devil with their behavior, and their life is going to work out OK. It won't.

The sad state of much of end-times Christianity is that there has been a huge departure from God's true call to salvation in many pulpits today. They preach a "way of salvation" that is devoid of God's call for mankind to repent and obey the Lord. Consequently, there is now in many churches a huge "falling away" from, and a corruption of, the original message of Jesus Christ and the Apostles to mankind, the one that says that we must:

"Repent (for forgiveness of our sins) for the kingdom of Heaven is at hand". Matthew. 4:17 KJV paraphrased

"And they went out, and preached that men should repent. And they cast out many devils, and anointed with oil many that were sick, and healed them." Mark 6:12-13 KJV

"Then Peter said to them, "Repent, and let every one of you be baptized in the name of Jesus Christ for the remission of sins; and you shall receive the gift of the Holy Spirit. For the promise is to you and to your children, and to all who are afar off, as many as the Lord our God will call." And with many other words he testified and exhorted them, saying, "Be saved from this perverse generation." Acts 2:38-40 NKJV

Of course, with a falling away from the preaching of REPENTANCE, plus confusion among professing Christians regarding what Jesus meant when He preached, "Repent," it is only logical that there would also be a fulfilment of another of the Bible's prophecies, that IN THE LAST DAYS there would be a famine in the land, not for food, but for the Word of the Lord:

Behold, the days come, saith the Lord God, that I will send a famine in the land, not a famine of bread, nor a thirst for water, but of hearing the words of the Lord AMOS 8:11 KJV

This failure to preach the entire Word of God is what is producing a great falling away among professing Christians. Their lives are full of tribulation, anger, sorrow, depression and sin, and there is little or no good fruit in their life, which only comes as the result of walking in repentance and obedience to God.

Just as God's Word says, the world in the last days would be filled with UNGODLY behavior. I know that we went over this passage at the beginning of this book, but it bears repeating here in a different version:

But know this, that in the last days perilous times will come: For men will be lovers of themselves, lovers of money, boasters, proud, blasphemers, disobedient to parents, unthankful, unholy, unloving, unforgiving, slanderers, without self-control, brutal, despisers of good, traitors, headstrong, haughty, lovers of pleasure rather than lovers of God, having a form of godliness but denying its power. And from such people turn away! For of this sort are those who creep into households and make captives of gullible women loaded down with sins, led away by various lusts, always learning and never able to come to the knowledge of the truth. 2 Timothy 3:1-7 NKJV

Before writing this book, I spent quite a lot of time seeking the Lord about which topic to write about. What is the most important thing for humanity in general, and the churches in particular, to know in these last days?

After living through the Covid 19 pandemic and the worldwide fear that it has generated, plus all of the global political upheaval of the present times, I believe the Lord has impressed upon me that we are indeed now living in the "perilous times" that Paul spoke of.

Due to of a lack of preaching of the truth, many people today really need to have a more accurate knowledge of God, Jesus, and the way to salvation NOW, for the time remaining is short. God is about to move His church out of the way. Once that happens, the wrath and judgement of God is going to fall on mankind one last time for the purpose of allowing the unrepentant one last opportunity for repentance and salvation, although it will be in the midst of great Tribulation and persecution.

For the law was not intended for people who do what is

right. It is for people who are lawless and rebellious, who are ungodly and sinful, who consider nothing sacred and defile what is holy, who kill their father or mother or commit other murders. 1Timothy 1:9-10 NLT

For God so loved the world that He gave His only begotten Son, that whoever believes in Him should not perish but have everlasting life. For God did not send His Son into the world to condemn the world, but that the world through Him might be saved. "He who believes in Him is not condemned; but he who does not believe is condemned already, because he has not believed in the name of the only begotten Son of God. And this is the condemnation, that the light has come into the world, and men loved darkness rather than light, because their deeds were evil. For everyone practicing evil hates the light and does not come to the light, lest his deeds should be exposed. But he who does the truth comes to the light, that his deeds may be clearly seen, that they have been done in God." John 3:16-21 NKJV

Jesus answered and said to them, "Those who are well have no need of a physician, but those who are sick. I have not come to call *the* righteous, but sinners, to repentance. "Luke 5:31-32 NKJV

God's purpose for the church is not to deceive people by telling them that all they have to do is take the wide road of just "believing in Jesus" and everything is going to be OK between them and God. This is not the truth, and it is not what Jesus preached.

Our responsibility as Christian leaders is, first of all to

repent and follow Christ ourselves, and then to preach the same message that Jesus and the Apostles preached to the rest of humanity calling sinners to repentance toward God and faith in Jesus Christ.

How I kept back nothing that was helpful, but proclaimed it to you, and taught you publicly and from house to house, testifying to Jews, and also to Greeks, repentance toward God and faith toward our Lord Jesus Christ. Acts 20:20-21 NKJV

My dear reader, I am telling you that it is almost "midnight" in Christ's prophetic timetable, and God is beginning once again to raise up His servants all round the world as voices in the wilderness to warn mankind in general, and the churches in particular, to "LISTEN to what the Spirit and the Bride are saying to the churches, "Repent and make yourselves ready, for the Bridegroom is coming soon".

It Is Not What We Know, But Who We Know That Saves Us!

I have made it no secret that I believe there are plenty of indications in Scripture that Jesus will return to remove the church, His Bride before the seven year Tribulation begins, but it might surprise you to hear that the primary purpose of this book is not to try to demand (or even necessarily convince) every believer to agree with me on WHEN Jesus will come to rapture/resurrect those who believe in Him.

In fact, I am quite confident that other Christians and I can be in disagreement about the timing of the Resurrection and we can still all go to Heaven. We can even ALL be wrong about exactly how and when Jesus is coming back and still go with Him because it is not WHAT we know about Jesus that saves us. It is WHO we have a relationship with and who we have decided to follow. Is it Jesus Christ, or Satan?

My primary goal is to help bring every reader to a closer walk with God NOW and make sure that we all have a firm Biblical foundation of the fact that God warns us that not every person who claims to be a Christian and names the name of Jesus is going to go with Him when He does come to receive His Bride up to Heaven.

I have written this book to teach the truth, not be patted on the back for lying to people. When Jesus returns, it will not be our understanding of eschatology (the study of end time events) that will determine whether we go with Him or not. Neither will our salvation be based upon any good works that we have done.

Jesus Himself declared that whether or not we go with Him to His Father's House will be determined by who we are following in our lives when Jesus returns for those who love Him. My deepest desire is not that everyone agrees with me on when the resurrection will occur, but that whenever it does occur, we shall all be following Jesus and all be caught up to be with Him, and so shall we ever be with the Lord.

As far as the timing of the Rapture goes, and if the reader is just unable to accept that there will be a pre-tribulation rapture, that's perfectly OK with me. I can live with that. We are still brothers and sisters in Christ. To be a little tongue in cheek about it, let us both repent of our sins and live for Jesus

NOW, and if I am right, maybe I will have an opportunity to explain it again on the way up. If not, I will be one of the first to ask advice about what we should do next.

If we are ALL living for God, and there is a pre-tribulation rapture, Jesus will recognize us and call us to come up to be with Him regardless of our opinion of when it is all supposed to happen, but if we are working iniquity in our lives, having chosen to keep following the devil in evil behavior, God declares that we simply will not be going with Him WHENEVER He shows up, because Jesus Himself has said:

Not everyone that saith unto me, Lord, Lord, shall enter into the kingdom of heaven; but he that doeth the will of my Father which is in heaven. Many will say to me in that day, Lord, Lord, have we not prophesied in thy name? And in thy name have cast out devils? And in thy name done many wonderful works? And then will I profess unto them, I never knew you: depart from me, ye that work iniquity. Matthew 7:21-23 KJV

Once we truly begin to know the heart of God and grasp the foundational Bible teaching that the Tribulation is not God's seven year "torture-test" for the righteous, but God's last warning for the wicked to repent before all who oppose God are killed and sent to hell and the Lake of Fire, I believe we can rest in hope as virgins waiting for our Bridegroom to take us to His Father's House.

We can believe Father God's promise that He has not appointed the beloved Bride of His Son Jesus Christ to suffer through seven years of severe wrath that God has already said is reserved for the wicked, not for those whom God loves.

Instead, God has appointed us to obtain salvation, merciful grace, and everlasting life through Jesus Christ. In the next chapter, we'll go over 1 Thessalonians 5, where God tells us through the Apostle Paul that the wicked are in the dark about such things.

It's true. Many people in this midnight hour mistakenly think a time of world peace is coming during the first half of the Tribulation, but that is not what the Bible teaches. God's Word says that through craft (deception) and the promise of peace, the Antichrist will destroy many. He will go forth conquering, and not long after the beginning of the Tribulation, more than one quarter the world's population will already be dead.

And through his policy also he shall cause craft to prosper in his hand; and he shall magnify himself in his heart, and by peace shall destroy many: he shall also stand up against the Prince of princes; but he shall be broken without hand. Daniel 8:25 KJV

And I saw, and behold a white horse: and he that sat on him had a bow; and a crown was given unto him: and he went forth **conquering,** and to conquer. And when he had opened the second seal, I heard the second beast say, Come and see. And there went out another horse that was red: and power was given to him that sat thereon to take peace from the earth, and that they should kill one another: and there was given unto him a great sword. And when he had opened the third seal, I heard the third beast say, Come and see. And I beheld, and lo a black horse; and he that sat on him had a pair of balances in his hand. And I heard a voice in the midst of the four beasts say, A measure of wheat for a penny, and three measures of barley for a penny; and see thou hurt not the oil and the wine. And when he had opened the fourth seal, I heard the voice of the fourth beast say, "Come and see." And I looked, and behold a pale horse: and his name that sat on him was Death, and Hell followed with him. And power was given unto them over **the fourth part of the earth,** to kill with sword, and with hunger, and with death, and with the beasts of the earth. Revelation 6: 2-8 KJV

Sudden Rapture-Sudden Destruction

The Lord's unexpected return for His Bride is going to catch most of humanity unprepared, and they will not escape. But those who love Christ are not in the dark. We do not know the exact date of Christ's return. We know it will occur suddenly, unexpectedly, yet we are not going to be shocked when Christ shows up because we know God has appointed us to be saved, not to have His holy wrath poured out on us.

Therefore, as Christians we should be wise, stay sober, and remain alert as we follow Christ, looking forward to our blessed hope of His coming on that day, comforting and encouraging one another with God's promise. Yet, for the wicked, there will be no time of peace at the beginning of the Tribulation. God says they will be facing sudden destruction right from the very beginning.

But concerning the times and the seasons, brethren,

you have no need that I should write to you. For you know perfectly that the day of the Lord so comes as a thief in the night. For when they say, "Peace and safety!" then sudden destruction comes upon them, as labor pains upon a pregnant woman. And they shall not escape. But you, brethren, are not in darkness, so that this Day should overtake you as a thief. You are all sons of light and sons of the day. We are not of the night nor of darkness. Therefore let us not sleep, as others *do,* but let us watch and be sober. For those who sleep, sleep at night, and those who get drunk are drunk at night. But let us who are of the day be sober, putting on the breastplate of faith and love, and *as* a helmet the hope of salvation. For God did not appoint us to wrath, but to obtain salvation through our Lord Jesus Christ, who died for us, that whether we wake or sleep, we should live together with Him. Therefore comfort each other and edify one another, just as you also are doing. 1 Thessalonians 5:1-11 NKJV.

Let's break this passage down into smaller pieces to give us a better picture of what will be happening when the DAY OF THE LORD comes as a thief in the night. The first things we need to take note of is:

1. This day will come UNEXPECTEDLY upon those dwelling in spiritual darkness. They have no idea that a thief is definitely going to show up at their house.

2. Those who are in spiritual darkness are not going to be alert and watching for Christ's return for His Bride. They will be careless, backslidden, believing promises of peace and safety on Earth when the Bride will instantly vanish and sudden destruction is going to come upon them, with God comparing it to the sudden onset of a woman's labor pains.

These two hints alone should be enough for the reader to understand that THIS particular "Day of the Lord" is not talking about the same Day of the Lord that will occur when Jesus returns at the end of the Tribulation to set up His kingdom on Earth as it is in Heaven.

The general time in history of Christ's return to set up His kingdom on Earth will be able to be easily determined by those who come to Christ during the Tribulation. They will know from Scripture that Jesus will return exactly seven years after the Tribulation begins, and exactly three and a half years after the Antichrist invades Israel and sets up His image in their temple.

Neither will it occur at any time when people on Earth are enjoying "peace and safety". When Jesus finally shows up to put an end to Satan's reign, the whole world will be steeped in terror crying out to be spared from the wrath of God. Even before humanity reaches the MIDDLE of the Tribulation, the Scriptures tell us what the state of mind of most of humanity will be during the wrath of God that will be poured out on the wicked on Earth during the Tribulation:

And the kings of the earth, the great men, the rich men, the commanders, the mighty men, every slave and every free man, hid themselves in the caves and in the rocks of the mountains, and said to the mountains and rocks, "Fall on us and hide us from the face of Him who sits on the throne and from the wrath of the Lamb! For the great day of His wrath has come, and who is able to stand?" Revelation 6:15-17 NKJV

Is the Rapture going to occur during the first part, or

near the middle of the Tribulation, or even later than this, at the end of the Tribulation, then? Not by any stretch of our imagination does this sound like a time of peace and safety on Earth, and from there on, things are going to continue to get worse until there is almost no flesh left alive. Does that sound like a time of "peace and safety?" Does it sound like something Christians can comfort one another with? Of course not?

When Paul was talking to us in 1 Thessalonians 5, he was talking about the pre-tribulation Rapture, not his arrival to set up his kingdom after humanity has all but destroyed themselves.

Jesus said that NO ONE knows the exact day and hour that He will return for His Bride, and we need to keep ourselves in a state of constant readiness for His return until that day occurs. The sad reality is that there are many today who claim to know Jesus Christ, yet they are not ready. They are not walking in obedience to Him. They are NOT expecting Christ to return any time soon, certainly not before the middle or the end of the Tribulation, or they would have already repented of their sins by now and be fully living for Jesus as they wait in faithful obedience for His return.

Will Anyone Ever "Lose" Their Salvation?

This is a very real concern for many professing Christians. Many today live with an ongoing spirit of fear that when they fail God (and we ALL fail God at times) they have "lost" their salvation and they have to get saved all over again. No, they haven't lost their salvation! We DO need to REPENT once we become aware of our sin, but God declares that if we truly want to be with Jesus, there is nothing and nobody in Heaven or Earth that can ever separate us from God.

However, this does not mean, as some have been falsely teaching that (in spite of Christ's call for us all to repent) our ongoing evil behavior has nothing to do with our spiritual state, and once we claim to believe in Jesus, our salvation is guaranteed and can never be "forfeited", regardless of how evil our behavior is.

There are people today who like to use the phrase "You cannot 'lose' your salvation", but they use the word in an unbiblical way. Their very use of the word "lose" is deceitful, implying that pre-trib leaders teach that there are people who will unintentionally and accidentally "lose" their salvation and end up in hell. Not only is this a misrepresentation of what we teach, it suggests that man has no personal responsibility to God for our actions in life. The popular slogan of many who are steeped in sin today is: "You can lose your reward, but not your salvation."

This dangerous type of spiritual backsliding and falling away is only fortified by preachers who think they have the seven year time period all figured out, and have misled their followers into believing that they still have plenty of time to repent because the Antichrist's rise to power during the first half of the Tribulation is going to be a relatively peaceful and bloodless rule until Jesus resurrects His Bride at the middle of the Tribulation.

Still others are echoing the overly optimistic claims of the disciples at that Last Supper that they are prepared to fight and die for Jesus. They say they are ready to go through the whole seven year Tribulation, suffering and dying for Jesus before the end, if necessary. Brave words, but words are cheap, particularly from anyone who is not living for God now. The problem with all of these scenarios and suppositions is that they are unscriptural on several important points.

No, we will not accidentally "lose" our salvation, but we all have the free will to despise Christ's sacrifice, trampling God's grace and Christ's gift under our feet as we deliberately choose to continue to work iniquity and follow Satan, even though we profess to be followers of Christ, and God reminds us of the fate of those who do this. If God did not spare His beloved nation of Israel for unrepentance, He will not spare us either.

For if we sin wilfully after that we have received the knowledge of the truth, there remaineth no more sacrifice for sins, but a certain fearful looking for of judgment and fiery indignation, which shall devour the adversaries. He that despised Moses' law died without mercy under two or three witnesses: Of how much sorer punishment, suppose ye, shall he be thought worthy, who hath trodden underfoot the Son of God, and hath counted the blood of the covenant, wherewith he was sanctified, an unholy thing, and hath done despite unto the Spirit of grace? For we know him that hath said, Vengeance belongeth unto me, I will recompense, saith the Lord. And again, The Lord shall judge his people. Hebrews 10:26-30 KJV

You will say then, "Branches were broken off that I might be grafted in." Well *said*. Because of unbelief they were broken off, and you stand by faith. Do not be haughty, but fear. For if God did not spare the natural branches, He may not spare you either. Therefore consider the goodness and severity of God: on those who fell, severity; but toward you, goodness, if you continue in *His* goodness. Otherwise you also will be cut off. Romans 11:19-22 NKJV

My dearest friends, you can never "lose" your salvation as long as you really want to follow God, but we have to be wise and pay attention to God's warnings that we can throw it away by continuing to live a wicked life, refusing to listen to the Spirit of God and the Word of God. Together, let's listen to the Holy Spirit and not make the same mistakes that Israel made, for God warns us that we too will be "cut off" for deliberate continuing unrepentance, just as Israel was. Let us together be wise and live for God so that when Jesus comes we will be "caught up" and not "cut off" to share the fate of the rest of this wicked and adulterous generation.

The Rise of Antichrist

First of all, God does prophesy that (at the beginning of the Tribulation) the Antichrist will broker and enforce a seven year peace treaty protecting Israel from all who would come against their nation. Yet, although the Antichrist will be hailed as a man of peace, Israel's friend and hero, there is no promise anywhere in Scripture that the first half of the Tribulation will be a time of general worldwide peace and there will be no military conflict.

In fact, the Antichrist may very well have to use military force to compel at least some of the Arab nations to cease hostilities against Israel, and that may prove to create a real problem. The Book of Revelation says that just the opposite of peace will occur at the beginning of the Tribulation.

The Antichrist will immediately go forth conquering, with the goal of ever greater conquest just like Hitler did in WWII). Furthermore, his campaigns will take peace from the Earth, and before long, more than **one quarter** of the Earth's population will be dead. Does that sound to you like a peaceful rise to power for the Antichrist?

On the contrary, Scripture indicates that when everyone is saying, "peace, peace," sudden destruction will come upon them. In Ezekiel 13, God warns against false prophets who will go around proclaiming, "peace, peace," when there is no peace, and God's Word tells us that through deception and craft, by the promise of peace, the Antichrist is going to destroy many.

And through his policy also he shall cause craft to prosper in his hand; and he shall magnify himself in his heart, and by peace shall destroy many: he shall also stand up against the Prince of princes; but he shall be broken without hand. Daniel 8:25 KJV

No, the Antichrist is not going to come to power by virtue of his devilish charisma and political manipulation alone as many are teaching. Yes, I know full well that some teachers are claiming that the Antichrist (the first rider on the white horse) is only depicted as having a bow, and no "arrows" are mentioned.

They try to suggest that this means the Antichrist will only use diplomacy during the first half of the Tribulation, and that there will be no armed conflict, but we have already seen that this opinion is totally against what the rest of Scripture teaches.

Reputable Bible scholars agree that the Antichrist is indeed the rider who appears on the white horse at the beginning of the Tribulation. He will go forth "conquering and to conquer" when the first seal is opened by Christ (described in Revelation 6). Furthermore, the Antichrist's military activities will provoke nations, and almost immediately result in "peace" being taken from the Earth and war breaking out in many places very close to THE BEGINNING of the Tribulation. Let's read it again in a different version.

As I watched, the Lamb broke the first of the seven seals on the scroll. Then I heard one of the four living beings say with a voice like thunder, "Come!" I looked up and saw a white horse standing there. Its rider carried a bow, and a crown was placed on his head. He rode out to win many battles and gain the victory. When the Lamb broke the second seal, I heard the second living being say, "Come!" Then another horse appeared, a red one. Its rider was given a mighty sword and the authority to take peace from the earth. And there was war and slaughter everywhere. Revelation 6:1-4 NLT

Then Revelation 6 continues on to describe the opening, in rapid succession, of the next two seals. By the time the fourth seal is opened, over **one quarter** of the population of humanity (billions) will die as the result of the opening of that one seal ALONE. This is not counting all those who will have already died from the Antichrist's initial military campaigns (seal one), igniting the wars going on in many nations (seal two), plus the worldwide ecological disasters, economic collapse, and social hardships which these conflicts will certainly bring about (seal 3).

So, the truth is that there will be no PEACEFUL three and a half years when there is no wrath of God during the first half of the Tribulation. It is simply a vain imagination that is not going to happen.

In fact, the book of Ezekiel goes into considerable detail regarding one of the conflicts that will occur near the beginning of the first half of the Tribulation. Let's take a look at this in the next chapter, as the evidence continues to mount, proving that the first half of the Tribulation is going to be a very difficult time of wrath for mankind.

The War of Gog and Magog

In the Old Testament, the prophet Ezekiel talks about a future war which the Bible indicates will occur just before, or shortly after, the beginning of the Seven Year Tribulation. It will probably be a conflict involving Russia (plus their European allies and Arab allies from the Middle East and Africa) against Israel (who will be backed by the Antichrist). Some have suggested that this prophecy was fulfilled in the "Six day war" between Russia and Israel in 1967, but the conflict which Ezekiel describes will be far more devastating than the one that happened back in 1967 between the Soviets and Israel.

This is another message that came to me from the Lord: "Son of man, turn and face Gog of the land of Magog, the prince who rules over the nations of Meshech and Tubal, and prophesy against him. Give him this message from the Sovereign Lord: Gog, I am your enemy! I will turn you around and put hooks in your jaws to lead you out with your whole army—your horses and charioteers in full armor and a great horde armed with shields and swords. Persia, Ethiopia, and Libya will join you, too, with all their weapons. Gomer and all its armies will also join you, along with the armies of Beth-togarmah from the distant north, and many others. "Get ready; be prepared! Keep all the armies around you mobilized, and take command of them. A long time from now you will be called into action. In the distant future you will swoop down on the land of Israel, which will be enjoying peace after recovering from war and after its people have returned from many lands to the mountains of Israel. You and all your allies—a vast and awesome army—will roll down on them like a storm and cover the land like a cloud. Ezekiel 38:1-9 NLT

From this graphic description in Ezekiel, this could very well be speaking of the rider on the "red" (socialist) horse who goes forth at the beginning of the Tribulation to take peace from the Earth. Their attack will be followed by the Antichrist's and Israel's devastating response to the invasion.

Their victory over the invaders will be so swift, shockingly powerful, and decisive that only one sixth of the invading forces will survive, and the Scriptures seem to indicate that this will be the conflict which sends so much fear into the whole world that every nation will submit to, and swear allegiance to, the Antichrist as world leader during the rest of the first half of the Tribulation.

Therefore, thou son of man, prophesy against Gog, and say, Thus saith the Lord God; Behold, I am against thee, O Gog, the chief prince of Meshech and Tubal: And I will turn thee back, and leave but the sixth part of thee, and will cause thee to come up from the north parts, and will bring thee upon the mountains of Israel: And I will smite thy bow out of thy left hand, and will cause thine arrows to fall out of thy right hand. Thou shalt fall upon the mountains of Israel, thou, and all thy bands, and the people that is with thee: I will give thee unto the ravenous birds of every sort, and to the beasts of the field to be devoured. Ezekiel 39-1-4 KJV

While the Bible does not elaborate on what kind of weapons will be used in this war, the amount of the devastation, the speed of the victory, and the terrible economic and environmental damage that will follow in the third, fourth and sixth seal judgements strongly suggests that limited use of nuclear weapons, or some new military technology, could be utilized by Israel and the Antichrist to quickly achieve victory in this coming war of Gog and Magog.

This also offers a reasonable explanation of how one-quarter of the world's population will suddenly be killed when the rider on the red horse goes forth to take peace from the Earth. Does that sound like a relatively peaceful first half of the Tribulation? In the coming chapters, you will begin to see that even though the Tribulation will dramatically increase in severity during the second half, God's Word tells us that the first half of the Tribulation will not at all be a bloodless rise to power by the Antichrist being preached by many Christian leaders today.

In fact, there will be MORE people (more than 4 billion) killed, from many different causes, during the first half of the Tribulation than the remainder who will die during the second half of the Tribulation, and the Word of God does not give any indication to us that there will be a mid-tribulation Rapture of living believers.

The First Resurrection will consist only of the resurrection of deceased believers and the Rapture of the Bride (which occurs just before the Tribulation), plus the Tribulation believers who die during the seven year Tribulation who will be resurrected When Christ returns to establish his kingdom on Earth at the end of the Tribulation.

The Book of Revelation says that these deceased believers who will die during the Tribulation will be the members who will complete the "First Resurrection," those who will reign and rule with Jesus Christ during the Millennium. So there will also be no living believers Raptured at the end of the Tribulation.

And I saw thrones, and they sat upon them, and judgment was given unto them: and I saw the souls of them that were beheaded for the witness of Jesus, and for the word of God, and which had not worshipped the beast, neither his image, neither had received his mark upon their foreheads, or in their hands; and they lived and reigned with Christ a thousand years. But the rest of the dead did not live again until the thousand years were finished. This *is* the first resurrection. Blessed and holy *is* he who has part in the first resurrection. Over such the second death has no power, but they shall be priests of God and of Christ, and shall reign with Him a thousand years. Revelation 20:4-6 KJV

Yet, that does not at all suggest that God is going to stop evangelizing the remainder of humanity during the Tribulation. It is God's desire to win back the nation of Israel during the Tribulation. Therefore, the Lord is going to raise up 144,000 Jewish evangelists during the Tribulation. There will be 12,000 from each tribe in Israel, all preaching Jesus Christ as the Messiah of Israel and the Savior of all.

In addition to that, God will have His two prophetic witnesses preaching Christ for three and a half years, plus angels (messengers) speaking through the heavens (possibly a reference to evangelism via satellite) all calling on mankind to repent of their sins and come to Jesus Christ. Remember, God is not a cruel taskmaster. He is unwilling that any should perish. During the Tribulation, the Lord's desire will still be for all come to repentance and faith in Jesus Christ for salvation.

As for us, dear reader, do not despair. The Lord has promised that, in spite of the darkness we now see increasing all around us, there is hope for the future regarding those who love God. We can take comfort in God's Word that He has not appointed His children to be part of this coming wrath.

God has called us to obtain salvation by grace through faith in Jesus Christ, who will return soon to "catch up" those who are ready. We will indeed go with Him to His Father's House while the wrath of God is being poured out on this unrepentant, wicked and adulterous generation of humanity.

After that, the evangelism of humanity will still continue during the Tribulation until the last people on Earth who have the desire to turn to God and follow Christ, including the nation of Israel, do so.

As for the rest, the unrepentant and the wicked, their opportunity for salvation will be over. When Jesus Christ shows up to inherit the Earth and establish His kingdom, they will all make the mistake of ceasing their hostilities toward one another, and they will align themselves to fight against Christ and His armies, and they will all perish in the brightness of Christ's second coming.

And I saw the beast, and the kings of the earth, and their armies, gathered together to make war against him that sat on the horse, and against his army. Revelation 19:19 KJV

Then I saw heaven opened, and a white horse was standing there. Its rider was named Faithful and True, for he judges fairly and wages a righteous war…
Revelation 19:11 NLT

He wore a robe dipped in blood, and his title was the Word of God. The armies of heaven, dressed in the finest of pure white linen, followed him on white horses. From his mouth came a sharp sword to strike down the nations. He will rule them with an iron rod. He will release the fierce wrath of God, the Almighty, like juice flowing from a winepress. On his robe at his thigh was written this title: King of all kings and Lord of all lords. Revelation 19:14-16 NLT

There will be no Rapture then. There will then be no

one left alive at the end of the Tribulation except the small remnant of elect believers who will be honored and blessed by God to be the ones to repopulate the Earth, just as it was in the days of Noah, and we, the resurrected and raptured, will reign and rule with Christ over these and their huge multitude of descendants who will be born during the Millennium.

Chapter 6

There will be a Resurrection!

Will There Be a Rapture?

There are still a very few professing Christians today who are actively professing that there will be no resurrection, (the spiritual children of the Sadducees of Israel's history – see Matthew 22:23). They believe mankind will just continue as is for eternity, but the Bible does not teach this.

Likewise, there are also still others who argue that the resurrection has already happened (2 Timothy 2:16-18 KJV), but both of these teachings are blatantly false, according to Scripture. The vast majority of Christians today have studied their Bibles enough to know God states that there will indeed be a resurrection of both believers and unbelievers, both the just and the unjust.

Furthermore, we also understand that this resurrection is yet to occur, possibly in the near future. If one looks at all the prophetic signs in the Bible which are coming to pass throughout the world right now, this "great appearing" of our Lord to "catch up" His Bride could be happening very soon indeed.

If we look at the words of the Apostle Paul in his defense of the accusations being made against him by the religious community in Israel, and look at the words of Jesus Himself, they say this:

But this I confess unto thee, that after the way which they call heresy, so worship I the God of my fathers, believing all things which are written in the law and in the prophets: And have hope toward God, which they themselves also allow, that there shall be a resurrection of the dead, both of the just and unjust. Acts 24:14-15 KJV

Marvel not at this: for the hour is coming, in the which all that are in the graves shall hear his voice, And shall come forth; they that have done good, unto the resurrection of life; and they that have done evil, unto the resurrection of damnation. John 5:28-29 KJV

Wait a minute! If Jesus said that those who have done GOOD will be resurrected to life and those who have done evil will be resurrected to damnation, isn't that "salvation by works" and not by grace through faith? No, it is not. It is simply Jesus stating a fact. As I have said in a previous chapter, there are far too many professing Christians today waving the banner of, "We are saved by grace through faith and not of works" and they don't even understand what that Scripture means, or this one either.

We all know that every single one of us has done evil in our lives. If Jesus meant in John 5 that "every person who has ever done evil" will be resurrected to damnation, obviously none of us could be saved. What Jesus is trying to get through the heads of His audience is that if we refuse to hear and respond to His preaching and the wooing of the Holy Spirit for us to REPENT, FOR THE KINGDOM OF HEAVEN IS AT HAND, there is no hope for us.

If we continue our lives following in the same old evil ways, we are **not** going to enter the Kingdom of Heaven and we are going to be damned because we are **already** condemned in our sin, and have **rejected** Jesus Christ, our one and only avenue of salvation.

As we just read in Acts 24, there will be a resurrection of both the just and the unjust, and it is only Christ who justifies us. It is only by choosing to believe and follow Christ that makes us just.

If we ignore what Jesus says when He calls upon us to repent of our sins, and instead continue to follow Satan, we are still unjust and still headed toward the resurrection of damnation instead of the resurrection of life, regardless of whether or not we claim to be a Christian. We can do all kinds of good works. We can perform all kinds of religious service. We can stand on street corners or shout from pulpits that "We believe in Jesus" and "Jesus is Lord", but if we are unrepentant, if we do not heed, trust and obey the Holy Spirit's call for us to REPENT, for the kingdom of Heaven is at hand, it will all profit us nothing.

Christians Must Not Continue to Follow Satan

We cannot continue in evil behavior, remaining disobedient and unrepentant toward God and expect that our good works, such as claiming to be a Christian, or going to church, or giving to charity, or even performing religious service will make up for our continued disobedience and evil behavior to the point that we will be pleasing to God and the Lord will be required to save us.

In fact, God makes it very clear to us that, without repentance, we can never be pleasing to God. All of our "good works" are like filthy rags and cannot save us if we do not change our evil ways and follow Christ. God calls them "dead works" because those who continue to listen to and follow Satan instead of God are not alive in Christ. They are spiritually dead.

If we continue to live our lives in that way, we are no different than religious leaders, politicians, Hollywood and Hell's Angels who make a great spectacle of giving to charity and making toy runs while the rest of their lives are filled with evil.

The truth is that God is not going to allow mankind (including professing Christians) to continue to kill and mutilate millions of innocents much longer (from starving people, to genocide, to abortion, to mutilating children for the cause of homosexuality and transgenderism). God is going to put an end to it all, and it is going to happen soon.

How close are we to the Rapture? Mankind's cup of evil

abominations is almost full, and God is far smarter than those who try to use the subtlety of Satan to justify continuing in sin while they claim to be followers of Christ. The Lord who created and sustains all that exists in creation is not going to allow Himself to be manipulated by those who claim to be children of God while they keep serving Satan as their real master.

Furthermore, it is the continuing unrepentance of professing Christians which is also the cause of adulteries, homosexuality, child abuse, violence, divorce, and many other sins **within** the church today that are almost as widespread as they are among avowed unbelievers. We should also be aware, reminded by the lives of Cain and Judas Iscariot that it is unrepentance among professing believers in God which is causing the exponential rise of violence, insanity, murder, and suicide among professing Christians, those who claim to know God during these end times.

These unrepentant have been in God's presence and hearing the preaching of Jesus, and in these last days, they even have the written Word of God to guide them, but they refuse to depart from evil behavior until Satan eventually gains control of them compelling them to do even greater evils, ruining their lives and the lives of others.

How bad can this get? It can get so bad that the sexual sins of government and professing Christian celebrities and leaders are now being exposed on a daily basis. It can get so bad that there are multitudes of professing Christians RIGHT NOW, in this generation who are aborting God's offspring, murdering HIS children in their mother's wombs.

It can get so bad that many so-called Christian parents are endorsing the indoctrination of their children into fornication and homosexuality in the public schools, encouraging abortion, and even allowing the sexual mutilation of their own children in the name of transgenderism.

It can get so bad that mass graves of children are starting to be discovered in these last days from native residential schools that were supposedly run by "Christians", and the backlash from those terrible atrocities alone is going to increasingly cause more hostility toward Christians in general as the time of God's judgement draws ever nearer.

The truth is that soon all Christians will be feeling the wrath of increasing persecution by unbelievers because of those who were, and still are unrepentant, those who call themselves Christians, yet continue to be workers of iniquity, still following Satan with their evil behavior.

Right now, today, there is only one thing on Earth that is hindering things from getting much worse than they already are. God tells us that SOMEONE is holding evil back. Did you know that (from the very beginning) God Himself has been constantly restraining Satan's evil activities and hindering the amount of death and devastation the Devil can inflict upon humanity? If that was not so, we would have all been dead long ago.

Someone is Hindering Satan!

All throughout the Bible, over and over again, there is evidence of many instances where God does not allow the evil activities of mankind or Satan to go beyond a certain point. God has never allowed Satan to rule completely unchecked, not when God is passing judgement on His people, and not when Satan is determined to destroy the whole world.

Even though Satan holds the power of death and has wanted to kill humanity ever since he first stepped into the Garden of Eden, God shows us in His Word that Satan's power to bring hurt and death to our domain has never been unlimited. It has never been without restrictions and limitations from God.

The Bible reminds us that God is the author of all life. In Him we live and move and have our very being. Death is actually God's enemy (1 Corinthians 15:26). It is Satan who wields the power of death (Hebrews 2:14), but God who controls his use of it, and one day the Devil and death are both going to end up in the Lake of Fire (Revelation 20:7-15)

If the Devil had his way, Adam and Eve would have died the same day they turned away from God before they would ever have the opportunity to bear any offspring whose future descendent, Jesus, would be able to throw Satan into the Lake of Fire forever.

If Satan had his way, he would have killed Seth in the womb as his followers do with many of God's children today. Or Satan would have murdered Seth the same way he used Cain to murder Abel, the same way he tried to murder Moses and Jesus at birth. Yet, God would not allow any of that. God prevented Cain from doing further harm to his family by banishing him from their presence. It was God who kept Adam and Eve and Seth alive to bear more children for many centuries before finally allowing Satan to bring death into their lives.

Yes, Satan would have used his follower Cain to murder his own parents and Seth, but God banished Cain the murderer from God's family so he could do no more evil to Adam and Eve or their children. Even when the whole Earth became so corrupted that the world was filled with violence and murder and mankind's every thought was only evil continuously, notice that God still prevented all those followers of Satan from harming Noah and his family, the only ones left on Earth who loved and followed God.

We can read all throughout the Bible where God repeatedly interferes with and hinders Satan's attempts to harm and dominate all of humanity, or destroy the godly in particular. In the story of Israel, God protects the life of Moses, and then controls the elements, wind, fire, and water, to protect His people from Egypt.

Over and over, when Israel repented of their sins and turned back to God again, the Lord sent both angels and human deliverers empowered by the Holy Spirit to rescue His beloved Israel from many evil nations who wanted to dominate and destroy God's people. Then, when Satan influenced King Herod to try and murder the Messiah, God also protected Jesus from being slaughtered by coming to Joseph in a dream and warning him to take his family and flee to Egypt.

Even in modern times we see that all attempts by Hitler, Russia, and the Arab alliance to eradicate Israel and wipe them off the Earth have failed over and over again because God will not allow it, and He helps Israel supernaturally. The nation of Israel is still beloved by God even though they continue to be blind to the truth that Christ is the Messiah that they have been waiting for, while they continue to suffer for their own unbelief.

Why do you think it is that every single nation that has

attempted to take over the world and eradicate Christianity has also failed in the end? It is not because of our military superiority. It is because God has confounded the plans of the evil one, brought confusion into the ranks of those who follow Satan, refused to allow the wicked to completely take over the world, and God is still doing it to this day.

There is **one** reason, and one reason only, that the seven year Tribulation and the rise to power of the Antichrist and one world government prophesied in the Bible has not already come to pass. It is because SOMEONE is right now hindering Satan and preventing it from happening. In the beginning of 2 Thessalonians 2, the Apostle Paul talks a little about the coming of Antichrist, and in verse 6, Paul says

And now ye know what withholdeth that he might be revealed in his time. For the mystery of iniquity doth already work: only he who now letteth will let, until he be taken out of the way. And then shall that Wicked be revealed, whom the Lord shall consume with the spirit of his mouth, and shall destroy with the brightness of his coming: Even him, whose coming is after the working of Satan with all power and signs and lying wonders, And with all deceivableness of unrighteousness in them that perish; because they received not the love of the truth, that they might be saved. 2 Thessalonians 2:6-10 KJV

Since the language of the KJV is a little awkward on this topic, let's also look at what God says in a more modern version. The first thing we notice is that the meaning of the words "withholdeth" and "letteth" in the KJV are to "restrain" or "hinder." God is telling us that SOMEONE is preventing the Antichrist from coming to power and He will continue to do so until He steps out of the way, or (as it says in the KJV) until He is taken out of the way :

And you know what is holding him back, for he can be revealed only when his time comes. For this lawlessness is already at work secretly, and it will remain secret until the one who is holding it back steps out of the way. Then the man of lawlessness will be revealed, but the Lord Jesus will slay him with the breath of his mouth and destroy him by the splendor of his coming. This man will come to do the work of Satan with counterfeit power and signs and miracles. He will use every kind of evil deception to fool those on their way to destruction, because they refuse to love and accept the truth that would save them. So God will cause them to be greatly deceived, and they will believe these lies. Then they will be condemned for enjoying evil rather than believing the truth. 2 Thessalonians 2:6-12 NLT

Although this passage talks a little about the "man of lawlessness" (the Antichrist) and how he is going to be destroyed by the splendor of Christ's coming, I don't want to focus on the Antichrist right now. The important question in this passage is: Who is the ONE who is holding back the rise of Antichrist?

In the KJV it says HE and in the NLT it says ONE. We can see from this passage that God declares in His Word that presently there is a single Person holding back the spread of evil in this world we live in, so it is important for us to know who Jesus sent to Earth to represent Himself and keep evil restrained until He returns for His Bride. WHO is the only **one** in all the Earth who has the power to resist Satan and win?

Where Has Jesus Gone?

During the days preceding Christ's betrayal and murder, Jesus had already spent considerable time on numerous occasions explaining to His disciples that He had come forth from Father God (as the Word), and would soon be returning to Father God again (through His death and resurrection), even prophesying that He would be killed and rise again on the third day.

For the Father himself loves you dearly because you love me and believe that I came from God. Yes, I came from the Father into the world, and now I will leave the world and return to the Father." John 16:27-28 NLT

Then Jesus began to tell them that the Son of Man must suffer many terrible things and be rejected by the elders, the leading priests, and the teachers of religious law. He would be killed, but three days later he would rise from the dead. Mark 8:31 NLT

Then, on the night of His betrayal, Jesus made a special declaration to His followers to give them hope once He was gone. It was a special promise they could have faith in, something to look forward to in the future.

Do not let your hearts be troubled. You believe in God;

believe also in me. My Father's house has many rooms; if that were not so, would I have told you that I am going there to prepare a place for you? And if I go and prepare a place for you, I will come back and take you to be with me that you also may be where I am. John 14:1-3 NIV

If we really want to understand God's promises to us in order for us to have faith and hope for the future, regardless of the evil going on in the world around us, it is important to PAY ATTENTION to the context of the promise that Jesus made on that day.

First, we are to put our faith and hope in what JESUS has said, and be concerned if there is any contradiction between Christ's Words and what many end-time preachers and teachers are saying today. So just what did Jesus say in His promise to His disciples?

Let's read it again! Jesus said, "My Father's house has many rooms." In the KJV, we begin to see an even more accurate picture of what awaits us in Heaven when we go to God, "our Father." God's House is big enough that it actually contains not just rooms, but many glorious mansions, and Jesus said that He would go THERE after His death to prepare residences for us (to live in). Then Jesus promised that one day, He will come back to meet us in the air and take us WITH HIM back to Heaven, so that we may also be there and live with Him where He IS NOW.

If we believe what the Scriptures are saying, Jesus has gone to prepare living quarters for us in Heaven, dwelling places that we will be inhabiting for an extended period. Heaven is not going to be some overnight pit stop at a heavenly motel after a resurrection at the end of the Tribulation, only for us to make a U-turn and come back to Earth with Jesus the next day to depose Satan and take over rulership of the planet.

Have you got it now? This makes me want to shout GLORY! Jesus has gone to His Father's House to prepare mansions for us to live in. When He comes for us, we will be caught up to join Him there. On that resurrection day, Jesus will return meet us in the air and "catch us up" to be with Him where He is now. We will then live in the Father's House for an extended period with Christ while the wrath of God is being poured out upon this wicked, rebellious, adulterous generation of humanity.

Even then, God will still be a God of mercy, forgiveness and grace. The vast majority of humanity will not survive the Tribulation, but as long as there is breath in their bodies, there will still be opportunity for repentance and acceptance of God's grace and salvation through faith in Jesus Christ during those last seven years of Satan's dominion over mankind.

Although most of the tribulation converts to Jesus will not make it out of the Tribulation alive, God says those who do die in Christ during those seven years will become part of the First Resurrection with the rest of us and reign and rule with Christ during the Millennium. Even in His wrath, God is still a merciful God:

And I saw thrones, and they sat on them, and judgment was committed to them. Then *I saw* the souls of those who had been beheaded for their witness to Jesus and for the word of God, who had not worshiped the beast or his image, and had not received *his* mark on their foreheads or on their hands. And they lived and reigned with Christ for a thousand years. But the rest of the dead did not live again until the thousand years were finished. This *is* the first resurrection. Revelation 20:4-5 NKJV

Having said that, it must be realized that the close continuous proximity of Satan to humanity during the Tribulation and the increasing wickedness of human society will mean that demon-possession is going to become pandemic among unbelievers during those seven years, resulting in unimaginable violence and cruelty.

As God repeatedly warns us, almost all mankind will die during the overspreading of abominations that will be the result of Satan and his horde of devils being further confined to exist only on Earth, and in the First Heaven which surrounds Earth, during the last seven years of his reign over humanity. Therefore, it is important for us to know a little more about what the Bible says of this Devil, who is so intent on hurting and enslaving humanity.

Lucifer's Expulsion from Heaven

Many people are not aware that the Bible teaches Satan will eventually be cast out of all three Heavens. As Lucifer, Satan was originally cast out of the Third Heaven (where God's throne is) before the universe was even created. Ever since then, Satan's domain has been the Second Heaven (outer space), the endless expanse in which God then created the entire universe.

Satan still presently dwells in the Second Heaven (outer

space) and he does not want the resurrected believers to pass through his primary domain to the Third Heaven, so He is soon going to try to stop the resurrection, and he will fail miserably.

And there was war in heaven: Michael and his angels fought against the dragon; and the dragon fought and his angels, and prevailed not; neither was their place found any more in heaven. And the great dragon was cast out, that old serpent, called the Devil, and Satan, which deceiveth the whole world: he was cast out into the earth, and his angels were cast out with him. Revelation 12:7-9 KJV

Some preach that this is talking about Satan's original expulsion from the Third Heaven, but all we have to do is look a few verses back and a few verses ahead to see that this second casting out of Satan is different from the one spoken of in Ezekiel 28, where God describes Lucifer's original expulsion from the Third Heaven, when God renamed him as Satan, the Devil. First of all, this expulsion of Satan does not occur until AFTER the death and resurrection of Jesus (the child of Eve and Israel) described just a few verses previous.

And she brought forth a man child, who was to rule all nations with a rod of iron: and her child was caught up unto God, and to his throne. Revelation 12:5 KJV.

In verse 6, God then speaks of a time of approximately three and a half years when the woman (believers in Israel) who brought forth Christ will have to flee for the wilderness. Many people do not realize that when Israel rebuilds the

Temple in Jerusalem, it will not be for Christ. Israel as a nation still does not believe that Jesus Christ is their Messiah, and because of the huge resurgence of Judaism in Israel during the first half of the Tribulation, there will actually be much persecution of Christians in Israel during that time.

Then the woman fled into the wilderness, where she has a place prepared by God that they should feed her there **one thousand two hundred and sixty days.** Revelation 12:6 NKJV

In this same passage, God tells us that at some point Satan is going to be cast out (of the Second Heaven) and the dwelling place of the Devil and all his demons will be further reduced to the area of the First Heaven surrounding Earth, and the Devil will hate this. Knowing his time remaining on Earth is short, Satan will immediately begin with great anger to come against the remainder of humanity, and the Tribulation will begin

Therefore rejoice, ye heavens, and ye that dwell in them. Woe to the inhabiters of the earth and of the sea! for the devil is come down unto you, having great wrath, because he knoweth that he hath but a short time. Revelation 12:12 KJV

Yet, even in Satan's wrath, God has mercy. God's Word tells us that the Antichrist will then break his treaty half way through the Tribulation and go after the nation of Israel, but the Lord will make a way for many Jews to escape into the wilderness where God will protect them, but woe unto any

Christians or Jews who remain in the cities during the second three and a half years of the Tribulation, for the Antichrist will put all to death who refuse his mark.

Now when the dragon saw that he had been cast to the earth, he persecuted the woman who gave birth to the male *Child*. But the woman was given two wings of a great eagle that she might fly into the wilderness to her place, where she is nourished for **a time and times and half a time** from the presence of the serpent. So the serpent spewed water out of his mouth like a flood after the woman that he might cause her to be carried away by the flood. But the earth helped the woman, and the earth opened its mouth and swallowed up the flood which the dragon had spewed out of his mouth. And the dragon was enraged with the woman, and he went to make war with the rest of her offspring, who keep the commandments of God and have the testimony of Jesus Christ. Revelation 12:13-17 NKJV

It should not be hard to understand then, the reason that God does not want us to be here during those seven years is that evil will truly be pandemic and Satan will rule almost totally unhindered until nearly all of humanity are following him, and almost all the rest are dead.

Anyone who truly begins to grasp the horrors that will occur during the Tribulation will not be under any false delusion (as some are today) that it will be "Christians" who are going to be in political, religious, and economic power, ruling over the planet when Jesus returns at the end of the Tribulation.

I know of some professing Christians who now brag of

their influence, power, and wealth because that is their idol, and they foolishly think they are going to dominate the world during the Tribulation. They mistakenly think their wealth, political power, and religious leadership will enable them to "take over the world for Jesus" during the Tribulation.

Then they say with false humility that they will hand everything over to Jesus at the end of it all. Yet, this is nothing more than the delusion of those whose gods are money, power, and fame. They are going to find out that it will not be that way at all. Rather, the few Christians who survive to the end will be in hiding, crying out to God to have mercy, and praying for it all to end.

Once again, I repeat, there is not going to be any U-turn type rapture of living believers happening at the end of the Tribulation. It is just not going to happen that way because (according to the Word of God) those few believers who do survive until Christ returns to set up His kingdom will NOT be raptured at that time.

The "elect" remnant of believers surviving to the end will be continuing their natural lives into the Millennium as God's chosen who will begin repopulation of the Earth, just as Noah and his family did after God's judgement of their generation. Neither will there be any "partial"or "secret" rapture occurring before then.

Was Christ's Resurrection a "Secret"?

Next, let's have a look at the resurrection of Jesus Christ. Some say we preach the coming resurrection will be a "secret".

Did Jesus rise from the dead on the third day as He said He would? Yes! Was it a "secret" resurrection? Hardly! Jesus Christ's resurrection was an extremely public event. God tells us that there was a massive earthquake. KABOOM! At the same time, a mighty glowing angel showed up, rolled the stone away from the tomb and sat on it, and his appearance was so bright and powerful that the guards shook with fear and fell to the ground in a dead faint.

Early on Sunday morning, as the new day was dawning, Mary Magdalene and the other Mary went out to visit the tomb. Suddenly there was a great earthquake! For an angel of the Lord came down from heaven, rolled aside the stone, and sat on it. His face shone like lightning, and his clothing was as white as snow. The guards shook with fear when they saw him, and they fell into a dead faint. Then the angel spoke to the women. "Don't be afraid!" he said. "I know you are looking for Jesus, who was crucified. He isn't here! He is risen from the dead, just as he said would happen. Come, see where his body was lying. And now, go quickly and tell his disciples that he has risen from the dead, and he is going ahead of you to Galilee. You will see him there. Remember what I have told you." Matthew 28:1-7 NLT

Some who consider themselves intellectuals have suggested that Jesus never really rose from the dead and that His sightings were something like a form of mass hysteria where his disciples wanted so much for it to be true that they just "imagined" seeing Jesus after His death.

The problem with that line of reasoning is that the mindset of the soldiers present, and the disciples themselves at the time of Christ's resurrection, was totally opposite from any expectation that Jesus would actually rise from the dead.

The soldiers were only there to prevent anyone from stealing Christ's body and "claiming" He was resurrected, and the disciples were all in tremendous sorrow and despair at Christ's death because (at that point in time) none of them actually believed that Jesus would or could come back from the dead after His crucifixion. They were all there watching as the soldier shoved a spear through his heart to make sure Christ was dead before they took Him down from the cross.

The disciples just did not have the faith to believe that Jesus would come back to life. Even after the eleven disciples heard the women's testimony of His resurrection, and after two other disciples had told the eleven that they had seen Jesus alive, they still did not believe the testimony of the others until Jesus Himself appeared in their midst at dinner time and rebuked them for not believing those who had already seen Him. You see, none of this in any way suggests that Christ's resurrection was a "secret" event or that it was the product of any mass hysterical illusion by people as a result of them all wanting and believing it to be true.

After Jesus rose from the dead early on Sunday morning, the first person who saw him was Mary Magdalene, the woman from whom he had cast out seven demons. She went to the disciples, who were grieving and weeping, and told them what had happened. But when she told them that Jesus was alive and she had seen him, they didn't believe her. Afterward he appeared in a different form to two of his followers who were walking from Jerusalem into the country. They rushed back to tell the others, but no one believed them. Still later he appeared to the eleven disciples as they were eating together. He rebuked them for their stubborn unbelief because they refused to believe those who had seen him after he had been raised from the dead. Mark 16:9-14 NLT

In fact, the eleven disciples were still so blinded by their unbelief that they could not accept that Christ had risen from the dead even when they saw Jesus after He teleported into their locked dining room and materialized in front of them.

At first, they thought they were seeing a ghost. It was not until they talked with Jesus, and He encouraged them to touch Him and eat with Him, that they finally realized and believed that it really was Jesus, and that He had risen from the dead.

Then the two from Emmaus told their story of how Jesus had appeared to them as they were walking along the road, and how they had recognized him as he was breaking the bread. And just as they were telling about it, Jesus himself was suddenly standing there among them. "Peace be with you," he said. But the whole group was startled and frightened, thinking they were seeing a ghost! "Why are you frightened?" he asked. "Why are your hearts filled with doubt? Look at my hands. Look at my feet. You can see that it's really me. Touch me and make sure that I am not a ghost, because ghosts don't have bodies, as you see that I do." As he spoke, he showed them his hands and his feet. Still they stood there in disbelief, filled with joy and wonder. Then he asked them, "Do you have anything here to eat?" They gave him a piece of broiled fish, and he ate it as they watched.

The Bridegroom is Returning

Luke 24:35-43 NLT

One of the twelve disciples, Thomas (nicknamed the Twin), was not with the others when Jesus came. They told him, "We have seen the Lord!" But he replied, "I won't believe it unless I see the nail wounds in his hands, put my fingers into them, and place my hand into the wound in his side." Eight days later the disciples were together again, and this time Thomas was with them. The doors were locked; but suddenly, as before, Jesus was standing among them. "Peace be with you," he said. Then he said to Thomas, "Put your finger here, and look at my hands. Put your hand into the wound in my side. Don't be faithless any longer. Believe!" "My Lord and my God!" Thomas exclaimed. Then Jesus told him, "You believe because you have seen me. Blessed are those who believe without seeing me." John 20:24-29 NLT

The truth is that nothing about Christ's resurrection was a secret. It was foretold by the prophets. It was prophesied to the very day by Jesus Himself. It was accompanied by a mighty earthquake and attended by an angel whose presence was so astonishing that it caused hardened soldiers to fall to the ground in fear. Furthermore, it was the SOLDIERS, not the disciples, who reported the resurrection to all of the religious and political rulers of that generation, and were then bribed to lie about it and say it did not happen.

As the women were on their way, some of the guards went into the city and told the leading priests what had happened. A meeting with the elders was called, and they decided to give the soldiers a large bribe. They told the soldiers, "You must say, 'Jesus' disciples came during the night while we were sleeping, and they stole his body.' If the governor hears about it, we'll stand up for you so you won't get in trouble." So the guards accepted the bribe and said what they were told to say. Their story spread widely among the Jews, and they still tell it today. Matthew 28:11-15 NLT

Then there is also the testimony recorded in the Bible, speaking of Jesus appearing after his resurrection to many others. This was not to just a few disciples on one occasion, but to hundreds over an extended period of time. Furthermore, the Bible records that the last person to whom Jesus directly appeared was the Pharisee, Saul.

I passed on to you what was most important and what had also been passed on to me. Christ died for our sins, just as the Scriptures said. He was buried, and he was raised from the dead on the third day, just as the Scriptures said. He was seen by Peter and then by the Twelve. After that, he was seen by more than 500 of his followers at one time, most of whom are still alive, though some have died. Then he was seen by James and later by all the apostles. Last of all, as though I had been born at the wrong time, I also saw him. For I am the least of all the apostles. In fact, I'm not even worthy to be called an apostle after the way I persecuted God's church. 1 Corinthians 15:3-9 NLT

This guy, Saul, not only did not believe in Jesus or His resurrection. At the time he saw the Lord on the Damascus road, Saul was one of the primary and most zealous unbelievers of his generation, a dedicated persecutor of the early church, who was intensely devoted to imprisoning Christians and having them put to death.

Yet, after a personal encounter with the resurrected Jesus on the Damascus road, Saul's beliefs were changed immediately and forever, and he is now known as the Apostle Paul, one of the greatest evangelists in history, and responsible for the inspired writing of almost half of the New Testament of the Bible.

Also, we have the testimony of the eleven disciples who witnessed Christ's final ascension back to Father God in Heaven, and again, it was no "secret." Rather, Christ simply rose to Heaven in front of his followers in a manner that was totally visible to all who were in attendance when it happened. If others had been present there, they obviously would have seen it too. In fact, if people back then had cell phones, it would have been all over the internet in minutes.

And he led them out as far as to Bethany, and he lifted up his hands, and blessed them. And it came to pass, while he blessed them, he was parted from them, and carried up into heaven. And they worshipped him, and returned to Jerusalem with great joy Luke 24:50-52 KJV

Chapter 7

Will There Be A "Secret" Rapture?

Are All Believers Raptured Together?

Most Christians agree that there will indeed be a resurrection, but one of the annoyingly common misconceptions promoted by those who reject the possibility of a "pre-tribulation" rapture is that many opponents keep insisting that pre-tribulationists teach a partial "secret" rapture consisting of only "good" Christians. They accuse us of teaching that there will be genuine professing Christians who are still saved, but will be left behind to endure the Tribulation with the unsaved due to their sinful behavior.

Yes, there are a few who do teach that, but the vast majority of us who teach the pre-tribulation rapture are quite clear that we believe that ALL who are saved will go in the Rapture, and all who do not go in the Rapture are NOT saved at that point in their lives because they are still unrepentant, still working iniquity, still following Satan. We teach that, regardless of whether or not people SAY they believe in Jesus or profess to be Christian, Jesus Himself will reply to the unrepentant, "Depart from Me, all who work iniquity. I do not know you".

Therefore, not only is the accusation that we teach a "partial" rapture of Christians a misrepresentation of pre-tribulation rapture (as it is most predominantly taught), the idea of a partial rapture is also unbiblical according to two important doctrines.

First, such accusations imply that pre-tribulationists teach the false doctrine of "salvation by works". Secondly, they also mistakenly assume that everyone who claims to be a Christian and believe in Jesus Christ is actually a Christian, when Jesus has already clearly declared to us that this is simply not true:

Not everyone that saith unto me, Lord, Lord, shall enter into the kingdom of heaven; but he that doeth the will of my Father which is in heaven. Many will say to me in that day, Lord, Lord, have we not prophesied in thy name? and in thy name have cast out devils? and in thy name done many wonderful works? And then will I profess unto them, I never knew you: depart from me, ye that work iniquity. Matthew 7:21-23 KJV

The truth is that there is nothing at all in Scripture saying that the soon coming "catching up" of the Bride of Christ (also known as the "rapture") will be a SECRET event. Remember, the resurrection of Jesus (the head of the church) was not at all a secret in Israel. It was a very loud and public miracle accompanied by a massive earthquake, brilliant light, the visible appearance of Angels, and eventually witnessed by literally hundreds of people in Israel. That is not a "secret" resurrection.

Is there any other precedence in Scripture which indicates that the coming "Rapture" will not be secret? Actually, there is. In the book of Revelation we are given God's prophetic description of the lives of the two witnesses, two prophets of God who will declare the Word of God from their headquarters in Jerusalem during the first half of the seven year Tribulation.

For three and a half years, they will preach the gospel of Jesus Christ from their headquarters in Jerusalem. God tells us that the miracles that these prophets will perform will be on par with those of Moses and Elijah, and their ministries will be just as upsetting to the wicked people of the world during the Tribulation.

Then, Revelation Chapter 11 reveals to us that God will permit the Antichrist to overcome Israel in the middle of the Tribulation and take the lives of God's two prophets, after which, the Antichrist will stand in the Temple, proclaiming himself to be God. At that time, to prove to the world that there is no such thing as a resurrection, the Antichrist will not even allow the bodies of the two witnesses to be buried.

He will require them to be left lying rotting in the street, broadcast by multimedia to the whole world, with mankind celebrating their deaths by giving presents to each other because these professed prophets of God who had so troubled the wicked of the world were now dead.

Oh, but wait a minute! The Lord has declared that death is not the end for people who truly love God. The Lord God who created Heaven and Earth has said that those who believe in Jesus will live and NEVER die:

And after three days and an half the spirit of life from

God entered into them, and they stood upon their feet; and great fear fell upon them which saw them. And they heard a great voice from heaven saying unto them, Come up hither. And they ascended up to heaven in a cloud; and their enemies beheld them. And the same hour was there a great earthquake, and the tenth part of the city fell, and in the earthquake were slain of men seven thousand: and the remnant were affrighted, and gave glory to the God of heaven. Revelation 11:11-13 KJV

Yes! Oh Hallelujah! The Antichrist will be broadcasting their dead bodies lying in the street to the whole world via multimedia and the whole world will be partying and celebrating their deaths, and SUDDENLY all mankind is going to witness a miracle, a mighty resurrection via live multimedia.

The whole world will be watching the two dead prophets of God when, suddenly, people will start pointing and yelling as the two men stand up on their feet again. Then there will be a mighty voice from heaven calling on the men to, "Come up", and the whole world will hear the sound, but they will not recognize the voice of God for fear. This will be followed by a massive earthquake which will cause a tenth of Jerusalem to collapse, and fear will come upon them all. Does that sound like a "secret" rapture to you? Of course not.

Now do you get it? Just as the resurrection of Jesus and the two witnesses was and will be very public, so also do the Scriptures indicate that OUR miraculous Rapture will be accompanied by brilliant light and incredible sound, and be observable by anyone who happens to be present when we go to be with Jesus.

There is nowhere at all in Scripture that suggests OUR coming rapture will be a "secret". Yes, when it happens, the event will be covered up and denied. Yes, it will be lied about, just as Christ's resurrection was. Yes, it will be explained away by the lying Antichrist and the False Prophet, whose whole agenda is to deceive the rest of humanity, but the coming resurrection/Rapture of believers will certainly NOT be a secret.

When we leave, with the light and the sound and the ground shaking, people are going to know something supernatural is happening. If they are in the presence of believers when we are caught up, they are going to see it happen, and the collateral damage from Christians suddenly disappearing all over the world is going to be massively destructive on Earth as well, particularly in the case of those who were controlling cars, trains, planes, dangerous equipment, etc.

Some people will argue, "What about The Bible's messages about the Rapture being a 'secret' and a 'mystery'?" First of all, the Bible does not say anywhere that the resurrection itself will be a secret event. What God's Word does tell us is that the IDENTITY of God's Redeemer of humanity (promised to Adam and Eve) had been a "secret" and "mystery" up until the arrival, death and resurrection of Jesus Christ.

Now to him that is of power to stablish you according to my gospel, and the preaching of Jesus Christ, according to the revelation of the mystery, which was kept secret since the world began, But now is made manifest, and by the scriptures of the prophets, according to the commandment of the everlasting God, made known to all nations for the obedience of faith: Romans 16:25-26 KJV

The Apostle Paul does say that up to that point in history the resurrection of believers had indeed been a "mystery," but the resurrection was a mystery that Paul was now preaching, explaining, and making public to all.

Therefore, since the Bible is now the planet's bestselling book, with more 5 billion copies of the Scriptures having been sold or given away worldwide, Paul's inspired revelations about the coming resurrection of believers can hardly be described as a "secret" or mystery anymore for those who want to believe the Bible.

Behold, I shew you a mystery; We shall not all sleep, but we shall all be changed, In a moment, in the twinkling of an eye, at the last trump: for the trumpet shall sound, and the dead shall be raised incorruptible, and we shall be changed. For this corruptible must put on incorruption, and this mortal must put on immortality. 1 Corinthians 15:51-53 KJV

Consequently, we already know from the previous passages that at the resurrection of the two witnesses there will be a mighty earthquake, a LOUD voice from Heaven "calling them to come up." Then, the two witnesses will visibly get up on their feet and rise to Heaven in front of the whole world (viewable both in person and through the worldwide media), so their resurrection is certainly not going to be any SECRET event.

Furthermore, this resurrection of the two witnesses also sounds very much like the prophetic description provided in the book of 1 Thessalonians describing the soon coming "catching up" of believers that we believe will occur just before the Tribulation begins.

First Jesus will descend from the Third Heaven with the deceased believers that He will bring with Him. However, Jesus will not land on Earth at this time. He will take up a position in the First Heaven at the edge of the Earth's Atmosphere, and then He is going to let forth a mighty shout.

For if we believe that Jesus died and rose again, even so them also which sleep in Jesus will God bring with him. For this we say unto you by the word of the Lord, that we which are alive and remain unto the coming of the Lord shall not prevent them which are asleep. For the Lord himself shall descend from heaven with a shout, with the voice of the archangel, and with the trump of God: and the dead in Christ shall rise first: then we which are alive and remain shall be caught up together with them in the clouds, to meet the Lord in the air: and so shall we ever be with the Lord. Wherefore comfort one another with these words. 1 Thessalonians 4:14-18 KJV

At the same time, the trump of God will begin sounding, and there will also be the voice of the Archangel (undoubtedly very loud if every believer in the world is going to hear it), and Jesus will command the dead to "Come forth."

It will be somewhat like the way Jesus called Lazarus to come out of the tomb after He had died. Everyone present at the resurrection of Lazarus heard Jesus call in a LOUD voice for Lazarus to "come forth" from the dead. Only this time, the Lord's voice will be so loud that the dead and the living of the whole Earth will hear it, and the bodies of ALL of the deceased believers in the entire world (the dead in Christ) will rise and be changed from corruptible to incorruptible, from mortal to immortal. Remember, after His resurrection, Christ first went into the place of the deceased beneath the Earth (Paradise), and released those who were still captive because there was no Redeemer until then. Then Jesus took the spirits of all deceased believers WITH Him when He went to Heaven. So, they will be coming back WITH Jesus at the resurrection to receive their immortal bodies.

First the resurrected bodies will be miraculously changed to immortal and incorruptible, and then those bodies will be reunited with every believer who once lived in them. Note that I said that it is the BODIES of the deceased which will rise, not the deceased believers. They are already with Jesus.

That is an important point to understand. When a person repents of their sins and comes to Jesus (by God's grace, through faith in the life, death, and resurrection of Jesus Christ) our spirits are saved from that moment on, and as long as we determine in our hearts to continue to follow God, no one can take that salvation away from us.

Even though we still now battle with sin in our bodies in this life, God says we are saved by His grace through faith in Jesus Christ. Even though our minds and thinking are still in the process of being renewed and conformed to Christ, we are already saved because of our faith in Jesus Christ defeating sin and death on the cross

Consequently, when Christians die, our spirits and souls now go immediately to be with Jesus, born again and made new, righteous, incorruptible, cleansed, and redeemed, when we chose to make Jesus Lord of our lives. The Apostle Paul said that he would far rather be absent from his body and present with the Lord, but for the sake of those who still needed Christ, he was willing to continue to live on Earth until the Lord determined his battle in this life was over.

Yes, by God's grace through faith in Christ, our spirits are already saved. Our souls (minds) are now in the process of being renewed and, at the Rapture, our minds WILL be perfected and our bodies will be redeemed as well. For deceased believers, the first two steps have already been accomplished. Their spirits are born again, and their souls have been completely redeemed. All that remains to be accomplished for them is the redemption of their body.

They are already with Jesus, awaiting the Father's appointed resurrection day, when we will all (deceased and living) receive the REDEMPTION of our bodies, and we will all be complete in Jesus. When we see Him, we will be like Him. When the living are "caught up" to be with Jesus and we finally SEE Him, evil will be eradicated from our thinking, and our minds too will become "very good" as our spirits already want them to be, plus our corrupted natural bodies will be transformed into incorruptible, immortal spiritual bodies, forever perfect as Christ already is.

For we know that the whole creation groans and labors with birth pangs together until now. Not only *that,* but we also who have the firstfruits of the Spirit, even we ourselves groan within ourselves, eagerly waiting for the adoption, the redemption of our body. Romans 8:22-24 NKJV

Beloved, now we are children of God; and it has not yet been revealed what we shall be, but we know that when He is revealed, we shall be like Him, for we shall see Him as He is. And everyone who has this hope in Him purifies himself, just as He is pure. 1 John 3:2-3 NKJV

Yes, when the trumpet begins to sound, the bodies of the deceased in Christ will rise first, and at the last sound of the trumpet, the last trump, we who are fortunate enough to be alive at that moment in history will also instantly be caught up to join them, so that WHERE JESUS NOW IS in the Father's House, we may be also.

There in Heaven we shall dwell with Jesus until Father God's appointed time for us to return with Christ to conquer Satan, the Antichrist, the False Prophet and all who follow them. Jesus will then evict them all and take over rulership of the Earth at the end of the Tribulation, and we will reign and rule with Him forever.

The Last Trump Controversy

One of the common errors made by those who insist that the Rapture cannot occur until Christ returns to establish His Millennial kingdom at the end of the Tribulation is that they will look at the mention of this "last trump" in 1 Corinthians 15 and insist that it must be referring to the same event as the "trumpet" spoken of in Matthew 24, where Jesus is clearly speaking of a trumpet that will sound to signal the return of Christ to set up His kingdom and the end of the world as we now know it, and Matthew indicates that the trumpet he is talking about will sound AFTER the tribulation and Armageddon. The common argument is that there can only be one "last trump", so they must be talking about the same event.

...what shall be the sign of thy coming, and of the end of the world? Matthew 24:3 KJV

So, let's have a look at Matthew. To begin with, in Matthew 24 we have a question brought forward by the disciples to Jesus, and that question was not about Christ's return IN THE AIR to "catch up" believers and take them to WHERE HE NOW IS in His Father's House. Their question in Matthew 24 was, "What would be the sign of His returning down to rule ON EARTH at the END of the world?"

In this passage, they are talking about a future event that will not occur until AFTER the seven year tribulation, when all humanity is in danger of there being "no flesh left alive," the point in time when Christ must return to put a stop to Armageddon, defeat and remove Satan, the Antichrist, the False Prophet, and all who follow them. Christ's arrival on Earth at that time will also be heralded by a trumpet, and after that trumpet, Jesus will set up His own kingdom on Earth:

Immediately after the tribulation of those days shall the sun be darkened, and the moon shall not give her light, and the stars shall fall from heaven, and the powers of the heavens shall be shaken: And then shall appear the sign of the Son of man in heaven: and then shall all the tribes of the earth mourn, and they shall see the Son of man coming in the clouds of heaven with power and great glory. And he shall send his angels with a great sound of a trumpet, and they shall gather together his elect from the four winds, from one end of heaven to the other. Matthew 24:29-31 KJV

Now, those who believe in a post-tribulation rapture tend to use the mention of the trumpet here as a key Scripture to be linked with the mention of the "last trump" used in 1 Corinthians and 1 Thessalonians to describe the resurrection of believers:

Behold, I shew you a mystery; we shall not all sleep, but we shall all be changed. In a moment, in the twinkling of an eye, at the last trump: for the trumpet shall sound, and the dead shall be raised incorruptible, and we shall be changed. 1 Corinthians 15:51-52 KJV

As I said, the argument which the post-tribulation promoters have widely used to support their assertion that the Rapture must occur at the END of the tribulation is that there cannot be more than one LAST trump.

Therefore, they contend that the Rapture must occur at the end of the Tribulation. While this argument may sound quite logical to some, that is because they have no understanding at all of how the trump or bugle was always utilized in Biblical times and how it continued to be used in military operations right up until the 20th Century to guide an army in battle.

The "trump" or "bugle," as it is sometimes referred to in more modern times, is a musical instrument which has no valves to change the tone of the sound coming out of it. Yet that does not mean that the trump is incapable of anything but a single monotone sound. Through changing the shape and pressure of their lips against the mouthpiece and the intensity of the airflow, an experienced bugler can achieve several octaves of sound from their instrument.

This is an important factor to understand regarding the

use of the trump for military purposes. When a commander wanted the army to respond in a certain way, it was the changes in tone, beat, and melody of the trump or bugle which signaled the whole army to move together in one accord in response to the different sounds that were being made by the trump.

The U.S. Cavalry, and later, the army, utilized the bugle in numerous different ways to command the troops to move together or to command to action different portions of the troops e.g. infantry, cavalry, and artillery.

There was a bugle sound to signal that it was time to get up in the morning, and there was a different sound to signal that the day was done and it was time to go to sleep. There was a sound to alert the troops to prepare themselves for an impending attack of an enemy. There was a sound signaling to attack the enemy, and a different sound that was used to signal retreat. There was even a bugle melody called "Taps" developed to honor the dead who had fallen in battle. As the Scriptures tell us:

And even things without life giving sound, whether pipe or harp, except they give a distinction in the sounds, how shall it be known what is piped or harped? For if the trumpet give an uncertain sound, who shall prepare himself to the battle? 1 Corinthians 14:7-8 NKJV

So the Word of God indicates that the trumpeter blowing the trumpet or bugle will cause it to emit different sounds for different purposes and each sound will be relevant to the action which is being commanded.

Now, try to envision this future scenario with me if you

will. Jesus appears in all His glory in the upper atmosphere of the Earth, accompanied by every deceased believer. Christ's arrival, being who He is (God manifest in human flesh), will be seen simultaneously all around the world amidst a light that will be far too bright for unbelievers to see who it is, and then the incredibly loud trump of God will begin to sound.

It will not be a meaningless BLAAAATTT, but a specific incredibly loud note, beat and melody that will announce Christ's presence and be supernaturally projected loud enough for the whole world to hear it. Yet most of humanity will not recognize the sound or understand its meaning. They will only fear and tremble at the brilliant light and the mighty sound.

Then the sound of the trump will change and at the sound of the trump, with the voice of the Archangel, Jesus will command the bodies of the deceased to "Come up" and be reconstituted, regardless of how they died or how much they have been decomposed and scattered.

It will not make a bit of difference if their bodies were burned to ashes or consumed by animals and insects, or sunken to the bottom of the sea. All of their bodies will **rise** and be instantly changed from corruptible to incorruptible, from natural to spiritual, from mortal to immortal. Then the spirits of deceased believers will all be reunited with their miraculously transformed, immortal, supernatural, spiritual bodies that they will then have forevermore, and they will never die again.

You see, when the Lord comes for His Bride, as we just read in 1 Corinthians 15:51-52, the trump will begin to sound and the dead in Christ must rise first.

Then, Paul says there will be a "last" (and probably

different) sound of the trump as Christ then calls on those of us who believe in Him and are alive and remain to also "Come up." At that moment, we will be caught up together with those who were already deceased, in order that we may all return together with Jesus to WHERE HE NOW IS, and dwell in His Father's House for a time, while the wrath of God is being poured out on the remainder of humanity for the last seven years of Satan's reign on Earth.

So the "last" trump of 1 Thessalonians 4 is not referring to the trumpet of Matthew 24. Rather Thessalonians is telling us that it will be the last trumpet sound in the sequence of trumpet sounds which will occur when Christ appears in the heavens to "catch up" both deceased and living believers.

It will be the final "trump" which signals that the time has arrived for all living believers to be instantly caught up in the air and join their deceased brothers and sisters, and ALL will be going with Jesus to the Father's House in the 3rd Heaven, and then the door to Heaven will be closed again and the Tribulation will begin.

Chapter 8

Post, Mid, or Pre-Tribulation?

Living for Jesus is the Most Important Thing!

For those of you who may not be familiar with these three terms, what they refer to is whether Jesus will be coming to "catch up" those who love and believe in Him at the end of the seven year Tribulation, during the middle of the Tribulation, or before the Tribulation begins.

Yes, it should already be obvious to the reader that pre-tribulationists believe, (as bad as things look in the world right now,) that the Tribulation has not yet begun. We believe that the last important world event to occur BEFORE the Tribulation begins will be the near-future arrival of Jesus Christ to catch up His body, His Bride of believers (the church).

However, it is of utmost importance that every reader understands that the purpose of this book is not to demand that every reader must agree with and convert to what we believe regarding God's timing of the Rapture.

To begin with, in spite of all my decades of research, I

don't know everything, so I could be mistaken about when Christ is coming for His Bride and I believe that it is little more than vanity when some people insist that only pre-tribulation, or mid-tribulation, or post-tribulation believers will be saved, when the truth is that, only time will tell which preachers and teachers have the better understanding on the topic of the end times.

The purpose of this book is not to make you agree with me regarding the timing of the Rapture. It is my deepest goal, not only of this book, but of all my books, and my whole life, to convince every reader of the importance of us all repenting NOW, living our lives for Christ TODAY, and dedicating the rest of our lives to constantly follow Jesus, being ever conscious of the very real possibility that our Lord could return for us at any time.

It could happen via Rapture, or we could simply die before Christ comes. It would certainly not be wise of any of us if we are continuing to work iniquity while we claim to be Christians, fully knowing that Jesus said that, in the last days, when He comes for His Bride there will be MANY who will be LEFT BEHIND claiming that they know Christ (see Matthew 7:21-23.) So, in my understanding, living for Jesus right now is far more important than whether or not we are right about when the Tribulation will occur.

Nonetheless, in the next few chapters I will do my best to present an accurate, fair representation of the post, mid, and pre-tribulation teachings which are circulating in these last days and offer some explanations from Scripture as to why I believe that some of these are not according to what the Bible actually teaches, plus the spiritual dangers of putting one's faith in any of these doctrines if our lives are not right with God.

Post-Tribulation Teaching

There are quite a few professing Christians today who believe that the resurrection of the body of Christ will not happen until Jesus returns to set up His Millennial kingdom at the END of the Tribulation. Furthermore, they do present some reasonable sounding arguments for their opinions and support many of their views with numerous Scriptures taken from throughout the Bible.

I also think it is important to acknowledge that many who believe and teach this position are mature and passionate Christians, whose salvation (I believe) is just as secure as anyone else's, for they believe that we are saved by repenting of our sins and relying on God's grace, through faith in the life, death, and resurrection of Jesus for salvation, just as I do.

Therefore, it is a foolish argument for pre-tribulationists to suggest that others are not or will not be saved just because we have different opinions on this particular topic. However, I wish that some of the post-tribulation crowd would have the same kind of grace toward the mid-tribulation and pre-tribulation believers and stop accusing us of spreading "doctrines of demons" which, of course, is untrue and insulting to the many other brothers and sisters who love and serve Christ just as much as post-tribulationists, even though they may have a differing opinion with these people on God's timing for this particular future event.

I will say, without any hostility, however, I believe that (in spite of the good intentions of most post-tribbers) their belief in a resurrection of living believers at the end of the tribulation cannot be true because it is in direct contradiction to some other important Scriptures in the Bible. So, let us delve into God's Word to see what the Lord has to say about the topic.

We already know that God does not lie or contradict Himself. Therefore, whenever I am confronted with someone preaching or teaching a doctrine which seems to contradict what I already know from Scripture and from history, I still do not immediately discard what they have to say. Instead, I think it is important for us to dig into the Word of God to see why there seems to be an inconsistency.

In the case of the Post Tribulation Rapture theory, it is based upon certain key beliefs by the Post Tribulation promoters which I will do my best to describe and then address one at a time as we progress through our study of the Word of God.

First, let's talk about the insistence of Post Tribulation promoters that all of the Apostles and early Christians were persecuted, imprisoned, and/or killed, and the Bible teaches that all who follow Christ and the Gospel are going to receive (great) persecution, based on what God's Word says in various places:

And Jesus answered and said, Verily I say unto you, There is no man that hath left house, or brethren, or sisters, or father, or mother, or wife, or children, or lands, for my sake, and the gospel's, but he shall receive an hundredfold now in this time, houses, and brethren, and sisters, and mothers, and children, and lands, with persecutions; and in the world to come eternal life. Mark 10:29-30 KJV

This know also, that in the last days perilous times shall come. 2 Timothy 3:1 KJV

For then there will be great tribulation, such as has not been since the beginning of the world until this time, no, nor ever shall be. Matthew 24:21 NKJV

These things I have spoken to you, that in Me you may have peace. In the world you will have tribulation; but be of good cheer, I have overcome the world." John 16:33 NKJV

And when they had preached the gospel to that city and made many disciples, they returned to Lystra, Iconium, and Antioch, strengthening the souls of the disciples, exhorting *them* to continue in the faith, and *saying,* "We must through many tribulations enter the kingdom of God." Acts 14:21-22 KJV

For, in fact, we told you before when we were with you that we would suffer tribulation, just as it happened, and you know. 1 Thessalonians 3:4 NKJV

Yea, and all that will live godly in Christ Jesus shall suffer persecution. 2 Timothy 3:12 KJV

Certainly, when you lump all of these Scriptures together and ignore the rest of the Bible and recorded history, it appears that there might be some credence to their arguments that God expects all living Christians to have to go through great persecution and tribulation during their lives in general, and during the entire seven year Tribulation in particular (or at least half of it), with many being imprisoned and/or being murdered for their faith in Christ.

The Scriptures do indeed indicate that many early Christians faced heavy persecution in their lives, and a great multitude of believers will have to face tribulation, persecution and execution during the seven years of the Tribulation, with only a small "elect remnant" surviving to the end of the Tribulation.

However, it is a mistake to form conclusions about the Word of God by only looking at a half dozen Scriptures without ensuring that our beliefs are not at variance with what the rest of the Bible says, with what we can find in history, and observe right now in the present world around us.

What is Tribulation?

Let's begin with making sure that everyone is aware that "tribulation" and "persecution" are not exactly the same thing. In the Bible, Jesus even uses the two words in the same sentence, a good indication that there is a difference in meaning between the two terms:

Yet he has no root in himself, but endures only for a while. For when tribulation or persecution arises because of the word, immediately he stumbles. Matthew 13:21 NKJV

To put it in a nutshell, "persecution" is opposition and hardship that comes upon us as a result of the hatred and evil actions of PEOPLE. "Tribulation" is a more general term which includes many hardships that are not necessarily caused by persecution (although they can be.) Examples of general tribulation might be sickness or physical injury, loss of a job or home, a broken marriage, the death of a spouse, friend or family member, etc.

Let's begin then by examining the word "tribulation" (which means hardships) common to all mankind. There were religious people in first century Jerusalem who were teaching, just as they do today, that if you are really serving God, your whole life will be relatively rosy.

Just as they do today, many contended that the reason they were wealthy, healthy and blessed and never wanted for anything was that they were the chosen of the Lord. However, Jesus exposed many of them as fleecing the poor to line their own pockets. Furthermore, many of these same people were teaching that if this is not your life, then there is something wrong with your faith and you are not a good person. They would even accuse the poor, sick, and infirm of being the worst of sinners, cursed of God, and Jesus deplored that.

I have even heard preachers in our generation tell people that if they weren't healthy or wealthy or healed or delivered, it was because they did not have enough faith, or they must have been sinning. Yet again, that is not what Jesus and the Apostles taught.

They taught that there is still evil in the world. Satan still has (limited) rulership of this world, and consequently, even as Christians, we will still all have tribulation. Furthermore, Jesus said the frequency and intensity of general tribulation worldwide is going to keep increasing until it reaches its apex during the SEVEN YEAR Tribulation.

So tribulation does not necessarily have anything at all to do with our personal spirituality or God requiring Christians to be here until the end of the SEVEN YEAR TRIBULATION. It is just something that all humanity has to endure, and becoming a Christian is not some magic talisman that is going to make all of that go away.

There will always be tribulation in the world due to the presence of evil, and in these end times, general tribulation is going to keep increasing in severity and frequency like a woman's labor pains until it explodes exponentially during the Seven Year Tribulation.

Just before Christ returns to put a stop to it all and establish the Kingdom of God on Earth as it is in Heaven, Jesus said there would be greater Tribulation than the world has ever seen, or would ever see again (See Matthew 24:21).. That is certainly a sobering statement when one considers all of the tribulation that has happened in human history and is still going on today in some parts of the world, but it will happen just as Jesus said it would.

What is Persecution?

Persecution is the type of tribulation and hardship which we experience as a result of a personal attack by another person or persons intending to cause us harm. Persecution can come in many forms. It can happen verbally, physically, socially, electronically, even indirectly. As Paul has already said to us:

Yes, and everyone who wants to live a godly life in Christ Jesus will suffer persecution. But evil people and impostors will flourish. They will deceive others and will themselves be deceived. 2 Timothy 3:12-13 NLT

Once again, this is not a reference to every real Christian necessarily having to go through intense violence, imprisonment and/or death via martyrdom. What Paul is saying here is that all true Christians are going to face general tribulation in their lives, and opposition (persecution) from people because many people in this world hate Jesus, and if they hate Him, they will hate us too. They will hate us because of what we teach, how we live our lives, and who we declare to the world will be their Savior and Judge, namely JESUS CHRIST.

Sometimes post-trib believers try to use the argument that Jesus, the Apostles, and all the early Christians were persecuted, therefore who are we to think that we DESERVE to be raptured before the Tribulation begins and not have to endure the same things? But hold on now! Wait a minute!

If we take a closer look at the Bible and at history, including what has happened in the last hundred years in Canada and America, it becomes obvious that what they are saying has not been entirely true for every Christian in every nation and every generation (any more than it was true of Israel in the Old Testament or the church in the New Testament.)

In the Old Testament God made a "covenant" with Israel, promising them that IF they continued to believe, trust, and serve God, the Lord would bless them and give them victory over their enemies, and they would be able to dwell in the land in peace. However, God also gave Israel many warnings that IF they turned against Him, their blessing would be taken away and their nation would be given over to persecution and domination by their enemies.

This is where many people today fall into great deception to their own hurt when they start twisting the Word of God and declaring that the promises of God are "unconditional" and irrevocable and that this means God would never remove the promise of salvation from His people for repeated unrepentance and disobedience, chanting the slogan, "We can never "lose" our salvation."

Here is where the problem arises. While God declares that His "love" for mankind has always been an everlasting love that is unconditional and irrevocable, we can clearly see from the Biblical record that God's Covenants (His promises to mankind) have ALWAYS been conditional all throughout human history as described in the Word of God.

All we have to do to verify this is to read the Bible from Adam to the time of Jesus, from Genesis to Revelation. The same pattern of God's covenants with man and the cycle of blessing and cursing is repeated over, and over and over again in the history of both the Old and New Testaments.

In the beginning, God told Adam and Eve that IF they continued to believe, trust, and obey their loving Father, everything will continue to be "very good." They even had the opportunity for eternal life. Yet, if they did not believe, trust, and obey God, they would die, but not because God wants to punish us for disobedience. That is just what will happen if we allow evil to corrupt us, because it is evil's very nature to consume and destroy all that is good until there is nothing left but evil and death, and our bodies will eventually cease to function because of it.

Later on, God spoke to Abraham and gave him the promise that as long as he and his descendants continued to serve the Lord, they would be blessed and be able to overcome their enemies, but if they turned from Him, they would be defeated and fall into bondage.

In the beginning, the nation of Israel served the Lord and He blessed them, but before long they began to transgress against God, and then tribulation and persecution came upon them just as God said it would, and their nation was conquered by nation after nation.

Furthermore that same pattern of repentance, God's forgiveness, deliverance, and then going back to evil again continued century after century until Jesus entered the picture when the nation Israel was once again sitting under evil, unrepentant leadership, and the whole nation was suffering both hardship (tribulation) and persecution as servants of Rome.

Therefore, we see from the Bible itself that the REASON Israel as a nation was being persecuted during first century A.D. was that most were not living for God. Consequently, they were under subjection to the heathen nation of Rome and to their own evil leaders. It should be no surprise to us then that those who were righteous in the nation were suffering because of the sins of the wicked:

When the righteous are in authority, the people rejoice; But when a wicked *man* rules, the people groan. Proverbs 29:2 NKJV

Yes, the reason that the first century church was under so much persecution was not because that was God's will or decree for every Christian to be martyred, but because the most prominent leaders of Israel at the time were wicked and hated Christ, and the nation of Israel itself was in enslavement to another wicked nation (Rome,) who also wanted to squash Christianity lest it led to a rebellion against Roman rule.

Nonetheless, even then, EVEN UNDER THOSE CIRCUMSTANCES, in the midst of all of this ungodliness, the Scriptures tell us that there was at least some period of time where not all Christians were constantly under intense persecution:

Then the churches throughout all Judea, Galilee, and Samaria had peace and were edified. And walking in the fear of the Lord and in the comfort of the Holy Spirit, they were multiplied. Acts 9:31 NKJV

Yes, read it again. God says that there was a time, even under Roman rule that the early church had peace for a time. The truth is that all real Christians will face some persecution in their lives because God's Word says that if Jesus did, we will also.

Nonetheless, the biblical record of Israel and the early church holds the key to why there has been little persecution against Christians so far in Canada, the U.S. and many other free world countries.

So, why are we not yet being imprisoned, tortured and martyred here as they were in the first Century? Why are we not yet being persecuted as will occur during the Tribulation.

If we look again at the Biblical history of Israel, we can

see that the Lord established His covenant with a godly man named Abram, whom the Lord renames "Abraham" (meaning father of many nations,) but God's covenant with Abraham and his descendants was not at all unconditional.

God told Abraham (and later told Moses the same thing,) that if he and his descendants and the children of Israel continued to honor and serve God, they would be the head and not the tail, and they would overcome all of their enemies and live peacefully in their land, but if they turned from the Lord, they would be brought into captivity and other nations would rule over them and enslave them.

Then we see that the way things proceed for Abraham's descendants is that God blesses them for a time, but they gradually began to depart from God and their leadership became more and more corrupt and wicked until God has had enough and He finally allows Israel to be conquered and enslaved.

Then Israel begins to cry out to God for deliverance until the Lord raises up godly leadership for them, who call the population to repentance and faith in God again, and when they respond to that call and repent, the Lord repeatedly leads them out of bondage to victory over their enemies and there is peace in their land again.

If you read through the Old Testament, you will see this same pattern, the same scenario, repeated over and over again in God's dealings with Israel. When Moses shows up on the scene, Israel is enslaved in Egypt because of their unbelief and sin, yet when they finally repent and commit to follow God under the leadership of Moses, the Lord shows mercy on them and leads them out of captivity. Pharaoh was ready once again to destroy all the firstborn of Israel, but God turns the tables on Pharaoh and leads His beloved nation out of bondage.

Then that same generation rebel again and again against God on the way to the Promised Land until God finally decrees that they are all going to die in the wilderness, and only Joshua and Caleb will remain alive to lead the next generation into the Promised Land to inherit the blessings of God. And so the pattern continued repeatedly with Israel with the last of Israel's overlords during the time of Jesus being Rome, and to Rome, the people of Israel had to bow in obedience or die.

So, we see that God's **love** for us is **unconditional,** but the covenants and promises of God are not unconditional. They ARE conditional. Neither was the persecution against Christians in the time of Jesus based on God's desire nor His will for things to be that way.

It was happening because the nations of both Israel and Rome, where the church first came into being, were ruled by wicked leaders, and there were many other people within Israel who did not know or follow God, and they too hated Christians.

That's WHY the nation of Israel was being ruled by Rome at the time. It was due to Israel's wicked leaders and their own unrepentance and unbelief as a nation, a continuing condition which still prevails in the nation of Israel to this day. Even though they do not realize it or accept it, the nation of Israel is still out of Covenant with God today because of their continuing rejection of Jesus Christ.

Yes, in these last days God has returned the people of Israel to their land as the Lord promised He would in the end times, but they are still suffering much tribulation and persecution because they still remain in blindness, unbelief, and disobedience to God and still reject Jesus Christ as God's chosen Messiah and Savior.

Consequently, because Israel as a nation remains in a state of rejection of God's Word, and because of their unbelief regarding Jesus Christ being the Messiah, there is still going to be a lot of tribulation and persecution ahead for them during the seven year Tribulation, as well as for all the rest of mankind who similarly continue to reject Christ and follow after the evil ways of Satan.

Modern Tribulation and Persecution

Now let's take a look at the modern world of the past few centuries. God has blessed those nations who have chosen to believe in and follow Jesus Christ, making Christianity the predominant faith in their nations, to the extent that Christianity has become the religion with the largest number of adherents in the entire world. More than 2 billion people today, worldwide, profess to be Christian

Nonetheless, across the globe, there is a huge difference regarding how Christians are treated, DEPENDING on the spiritual states of those who lead various countries, worldwide, and the beliefs of the majority of the population within those countries.

Where Christianity has become the dominant belief in a nation, God has blessed those nations, even in spite of the imperfections in many Christians and the leaders of the nations. For the most part, historical evidence indicates that

God's blessing on a nation as a whole is as much dependent upon who is in power governing a nation as it is to the spiritual condition of the general population existing in any particular country. They both play a part in the general acceptance, or persecution of Christians within the population.

As God has already told us in Proverbs, when the righteous are in authority, the people rejoice, but when the wicked rule, the people groan and suffer. All we have to do is look at the world around us. In the nations of the world today where the one true God and Christ are rejected by leadership and most of the population of a nation, Christians suffer much persecution because Satan is in charge.

No, our own nations are not perfect. Yet, all you have to do is look at the founding documents and history of the nations of Canada and the U.S. to see that, in spite of failing God in many ways, the founders of our nations established our countries upon a belief in God and following Jesus Christ. Those of us who are old enough to remember, can recall the entire country pretty well came to a standstill on Sundays in the earlier years of our nations, so people could attend church and spend time with their families.

For those who say that every true Christian must go through life-threatening tribulation and persecution to the extent of torture, imprisonment and death for their belief in Jesus, I have a statement and a question for you. That has not been the case in the free world for over a hundred years including in the lives of the people in Canada and the U.S. trying to promote these beliefs.

Are you trying to say that there have been no real Christians in the free world during the last hundred years? That is foolishness! We have been blessed in our nations due to our nations' and ancestors' commitments to God's covenants and principles up until this generation.

Listen to me, dear reader. The reason that we have not had to endure the same kind of persecution in our nations in the free world that has long been occurring in many other countries is because there has been a godly contingent of men and women in positions of power ruling our nations and (until recently) there has been a majority segment of the population who have always been Christian, or at least tolerant of Christianity.

For anyone to suggest it is God's will for all Christians to go through the kind of tribulation and persecution that is going to happen during the Tribulation as a result of God's great wrath against the ungodly is to totally deny and ignore God's Covenant promises to God's corporate Christian "nation" worldwide who love Him.

We are Christ's royal priesthood, God's chosen generation, His peculiar people, His holy spiritual nation, and God says that if our spiritual nation (of Christians) honors Him, we will be shown mercy, not wrath.

But you *are* a chosen generation, a royal priesthood, a holy nation, His own special people, that you may proclaim the praises of Him who called you out of darkness into His marvelous light; who once *were* not a people but *are* now the people of God, who had not obtained mercy but now have obtained mercy. 1 Peter 2:9-10 NKJV

Nevertheless, we cannot ignore that the God-fearing society and tolerance of Biblical Christianity which we have particularly enjoyed for the past generation has been eroding very rapidly worldwide during this most recent decade. It is becoming painfully obvious that the persecution of devoted Christians which is now beginning to mount in North America, is going to get much worse, not better in the future, if the Lord tarries much longer.

Why? It is because many of our leaders and the people in our nations today who say they are Christians no longer follow Jesus, and they hate those who do, just like those who claimed to be children of Abraham and followers of Moses when they persecuted Jesus and the disciples. So persecution of Christians is going to continue to worsen unless our nations turn back to God again.

How does all of this relate to the Seven Year Tribulation? Again, all of the tribulation that is going to occur during the Tribulation period has nothing to do with the warped idea that God is some sort of cruel Deity who is going to require His Son's Bride to be "torture tested" during seven years of wrath.

God has already declared that his WRATH is reserved for the wicked, not the righteous, and we are not appointed to wrath, but grace, mercy and salvation. What we have seen up to now is general tribulation and persecution increasing or decreasing in relation to the spiritual condition of each nation. It is not the wrath of God as described to be coming upon the wicked during the Tribulation.

What about the claims by post-tribbers that pre-tribulation believers are not prominent in countries where Christians are heavily persecuted? That is simply not a true statement. There are plenty of Christian ministries teaching a pre-tribulation rapture in these countries. The only reason that these people are not aware of this or do not want to admit this is that they run with the crowd who want to believe otherwise.

Neither does the teaching of a pre-tribulation rapture exist because (as some claim) those who teach it think that we are more worthy or entitled to go to Heaven without suffering the same kind of persecution that others are having to endure in the world. That is a ridiculous statement.

If anything, it will be an extremely humbling experience to come face to face with Jesus on the day when we see Him, knowing that there are so many who have suffered so very much more for their faith than we have had to endure. We know we are not worthy to be spared the Tribulation, and we know that if the Lord tarries much longer, a lot more suffering is going to be coming our way into the lives of Christians who have been living in what we would now call the "free" world.

Why will this happen? It's not hard to discern that if the Lord tarries much longer, much greater persecution of Christians will also be coming to our nations because the spiritual condition of this world is deteriorating fast. Many of our freedoms are already beginning to be eroded as the majority population and the leaders of our countries get further and further from God, and the more the ungodly get into power over the nation, the worse it is going to get for Christians until the Rapture occurs.

Our position on the timing of the Rapture has nothing to do with entitlement or worthiness of the North American church. Rather it is based upon our belief in God's Word where God says that there is a God ordained time for all things, and those who love and follow Christ are not appointed to suffer His coming wrath against the wicked and unrepentant of the world.

Consequently, the arrival of Jesus to "catch up" His Bride will occur suddenly and unexpectedly at Father God's appointed time in history, and is not at all dependent upon when mankind believes or wants it to happen. We believe that God is sovereign and He will do what He wants, exactly when He wants to do it.

Is Pre-Trib Rapture "New"?

I am not going to take much time to talk about the ridiculous claims by some that the teaching of a pre-tribulation rapture is a heretical doctrine that did not exist in church history until John Darby promoted a pre-tribulation rapture in the 1800's. To begin with, the statement is false. Anyone who wants to do some honest, independent research on the presence of pre-tribulation rapture beliefs in the early church can find historical writings, both pro and con, regarding a pre-tribulation rapture that go back to some of the earliest church writings that there are records of.

In addition, it should be irrelevant to us what John Darby, or any other 19th century preacher, or any modern preacher says about the Rapture. We should be formulating our doctrine about the Rapture from our own study of the inspired Word of God, not just accepting what any preacher has to say about it. Like the Bereans, whom Paul spoke of in Acts 17:11, we should be noble enough to be studying the Scriptures daily to make sure that the things we are being taught are true.

In 40 years of Bible study, I had never even heard of John Darby or what he taught about the Rapture until people started saying recently that belief in a pre-tribulation Rapture all started with Darby in the 1800's. What I believe and teach today about the Rapture comes from many years of my own study of the Word of God.

Yes, I have also listened to and intensely studied the mid-trib and post-trib views over the years, but when I compare what they are saying with what the Scriptures say, I cannot with good conscience teach what they are promoting, when I firmly believe that the Scriptures teach a pre-tribulation rapture. So I will keep warning people to be always "ready" for the imminent return of Jesus, and I will continue to do so until Jesus comes to "catch us" up, or until I see the Antichrist come to power.

I will ignore the wild accusations being made that all the pre-tribulation believers are going to "fall away" and be deceived by the Antichrist if the Rapture does not happen when we think it will. I wish people would stop saying such foolish things. If we find we have been mistaken about God's timing of the Rapture, we will just keep on following Christ the way we have already determined in our hearts to do in case He comes for us TODAY, already walking in the Spirit and best prepared for whatever lies ahead in the future because we are already used to the whole armor of God and wielding the Sword of God's Word.

Who will be Raptured?

This is actually a far more important question to know the Biblical answer to than WHEN the Rapture will occur, because it provides us with the explanation as to why there cannot be rapture of living believers at the end of the Tribulation. It also reveals why there will be no partial pre-tribulation rapture of living believers before the start of the Tribulation, or partial rapture of believers in the middle of the Tribulation.

First we'll talk a little about the word "rapture" itself for the benefit of readers who have been grinding their teeth every time I mention the word because they have been programmed to believe there can be no pre-tribulation rapture. After all, the word "rapture" is not even in the KJV Bible.

As valid a point as some Bible thumping preachers want to make this sound, this is really quite a silly argument about a word which is nothing more than a coined word from the original Latin words (rapio, raeptius, rapturo, rapturus) meaning "seized" or "grabbed up."

Thus, the word "rapture" is the exact description of what will happen to living believers when Christ comes for His bride. It is also a very good description of the intense pleasure and joyful state of mind that we will all have on the way up, so the fact that the word is not used in the KJV should really be a non-issue among serious believers.

"THUMP! THUMP! THUMP! go the Bible thumpers. "The word 'rapture' is NOT in the Bible, I tell you!" Fine, if it bothers you that much, use the words "caught up" found in the KJV description of the event described in 1 Thessalonians 4:17, but I wouldn't gloat over your point too much because there are a lot of other words that we use today which are not in the Bible either. Yet, they are perfectly legitimate synonyms for words or phrases in the KJV, and no one has any trouble understanding what we are talking about if they

164

really want to.

The word "dinosaur" is not in the Bible, but there is mention of the largest creature God ever made in Job 40:15-24 KJV which God calls a "behemoth". Yet, what God gives us in the book of Job is a perfect description of a massive land dinosaur who caused the ground to shake when he walked and had a tail like a mighty cedar tree.

"Look at Behemoth, which I made along with you and which feeds on grass like an ox. What strength it has in its loins, what power in the muscles of its belly! Its tail sways like a cedar; the sinews of its thighs are close-knit. Its bones are tubes of bronze, its limbs like rods of iron. It ranks first among the works of God, yet its Maker can approach it with his sword." Job 40:15-19 NIV

HINT! Ignore the Bible commentators and some modern versions of the Bible, where this animal is referred to as an elephant, rhino, or hippo. It's not! All of these animals have tails like whisk brooms. There is no massive land animal in existence on Earth in modern times that has a tail like a mighty cedar tree. God is talking about a dinosaur. Yet the word dinosaur is not in the KJV.

The word grandfather is not in the Bible either, but if I told you Methuselah was Noah's grandfather you would not have any trouble understanding what I mean and you would not be arguing with me about the word not being in the Bible.

In fact, the word "Bible" itself comes from the Greek words "Biblios and "Biblia", meaning "book" or "books". However, the word "Bible" cannot be found in the KJV Scriptures, but everyone knows what we mean when we use the word Bible. So if you don't mind, I will continue to use the word "Rapture" to describe what is going to happen when Jesus returns for His Bride, and those who object can delete the word from their mind and use the phrase "caught up," because both words mean exactly the same thing.

Now that this particular "elephant" is out of the way, let's talk about who is going to be "caught up" to be with the Lord when Jesus returns for His Bride, and on that subject, God's Word is quite clear to us about that. There will be no PARTIAL rapture of living believers when Jesus shows up. Every single person who is a follower of Christ WILL be going in the Rapture when Jesus arrives to receive us up to where He now is.

So, from that perspective, it does not really matter when we think the Rapture will occur historically. It won't matter what our theology, eschatology or any of our other "ology's are when Jesus does show up. The Bible is clear that whenever Jesus arrives, all true believers are going to go with Him.

Everyone on Earth who is actually a Christian when Jesus calls for those who are His to "come up" will be "caught up" in the air to join every deceased believer and we will all go with Jesus to His Father's House.

NOBODY who knows Christ will be left behind when Jesus comes for those who love Him. Therefore, if you are still here after the Rapture happens, it means that you DIDN'T pull one over on God. You did not get away with being unrepentant and continuing to follow Satan while claiming to believe in Jesus. You were not really a true Christian.

The Bible is very clear that when Jesus comes, there will be many who are expecting Him to come and are actually looking for His coming, but they are NOT going to go with

Him because, even though they claim to know Jesus, do good works, perform religious service, they are unrepentant (like Cain and Judas Iscariot) and insist on continuing to live an evil life, even though they know God is calling them to repent. (See Matthew 7:21-23 and Luke 13:24-28)

So how can anyone ever make it to Heaven? Certainly none of us are going to make it by our own righteousness or by doing good works, but, fortunately for all of us, God has promised grace for all who repent of our sins and put our faith in the life, death and resurrection of Jesus, for salvation and restoration back into God's family again. If we REALLY believe that, we will repent and we will ask for the Holy Spirit's help to follow Jesus, and we will also do good works, not because we have to in order to be saved, but because we want to.

It is not any preacher's place to judge the individual salvation of any believer. That will be up to God. Our salvation will be between each one of us and God, for only He knows our hearts, but that does not mean that God has given me license to tell people that it is Ok with God for them to keep sinning.

My responsibility as a Christian leader is to encourage all of us to repent of our sins and come to Christ for salvation, and set an example for others to follow. Knowing God's warning to me as a leader, I cannot shrink from my responsibility of warning the wicked, whom God says will NOT be going to Heaven if they do not change their evil ways.

Regardless of how much people may not like it, or how much persecution will come upon those who preach the gospel, we love the lost enough to bear that rejection and persecution when we know that it comes with the hope that, if we continue to tell all people the truth, at least some will repent, believe on Jesus, and be saved.

No One Left to be Raptured!

Now we have come to what I believe is the primary and Biblically indisputable reason that there cannot be a post-tribulation Rapture of living believers. Some post-tribulation preachers today are actually managing to convince people that "true" (their words, not mine) Christians are going to continue to gain economic prosperity and political power in the world until they manage to take over the world before Jesus gets here.

Then they think they are going to hand the government of the world over to Jesus when He arrives, and these people are getting rich preaching this stuff while they fleece their followers. I tell you, all of these people are going to be in for a very rude surprise when the Antichrist rises to power.

Many other post tribbers strongly believe that it is God's will for all believers to suffer through seven years of persecution and tribulation, prepared to be imprisoned, tortured, and die for Jesus in the future (the same way many Christians have already been suffering in heathen nations for centuries).

Consequently, many post-tribulation believers have bunkers, weapons, and survival supplies that they have already stockpiled (or are planning to.) They are preparing to barricade themselves in their homes, or hunker down in a bunker, or head for the wilderness when the Antichrist shows up.

Their hope for the future is that, in spite of the fact that almost all of the human population (literally billions) are going to die, they will be among the few who (with God's help) will end up being the "elect remnant" who will manage to survive to the end of the Tribulation. Does that sound like the same message that Titus preached?

For the grace of God that brings salvation has appeared to all men, teaching us that, denying ungodliness and worldly lusts, we should live soberly, righteously, and godly in the present age, looking for the blessed hope and glorious appearing of our great God and Savior Jesus Christ Titus 2:11-13 NKJV

In 1 Thessalonians Paul talked about comforting one another with God's promise of our Rapture if we are still alive when it happens. Yet, for the post-tribulation believer, their only hope is to try to survive all the horrors that are coming until the end of the Tribulation and be raptured when Jesus shows up. There's not much comfort in that. Also, in their version of the future, living believers will not be spending a lot of time with Jesus in Heaven.

In their view, the rapture will be a quick round trip to Heaven and back, heading up just to get our resurrected body and then making a quick U-turn right back down to Earth again to begin our millennial rule with Jesus. The biggest problem with this whole scenario is that these people have not really thought this out very well.

When Jesus returns during Armageddon at the end of the Tribulation, if Satan is bound and cast in the bottomless pit, if the Antichrist and the False Prophet are thrown into the Lake of Fire, and ALL the human population who oppose Christ are destroyed, as we are told will happen in Revelation 19:19-21, the ONLY ones who are going to be left on Earth will be living believers, and that presents a real dilemma for those preaching a post-tribulation rapture of the living.

If all surviving believers at the end of the Tribulation are going to be "caught up" to receive their incorruptible, immortal, eternal spiritual bodies at that time, we have a contradiction in the Bible. Why?

Jesus has told us that after we receive our resurrected/raptured spiritual bodies there will be no more marrying or giving in marriage (e.g. no more reproduction for us – we will be like the angels in Heaven;) neither can we die anymore.

Therefore, if all the wicked on Earth are destroyed and all living believers on Earth are Raptured at the end of the Tribulation, that leaves NO ONE left alive on Earth for us to reign over, no one to repopulate the Earth during the Millennium, and no one capable of dying during the Millennium.

However, that is not what the Bible teaches. What God's Word does say is that the "elect" remnant of believers who come to Christ during the Tribulation and survive to the end of it will be the ones continuing into the Millennium in their natural bodies for the purpose of repopulating the Earth. Under the rulership of Jesus and the resurrected saints, THEY will be the ones cleaning up the huge worldwide mess that humanity will have made of our planet up until that time in history.

And seven months shall the house of Israel be burying of

them, that they may cleanse the land. Yea, all the people of the land shall bury them; and it shall be to them a renown the day that I shall be glorified, saith the Lord God. And they shall sever out men of continual employment, passing through the land to bury with the passengers those that remain upon the face of the earth, to cleanse it: after the end of seven months shall they search. Ezekiel 39:12-14 KJV

And they that dwell in the cities of Israel shall go forth, and shall set on fire and burn the weapons, both the shields and the bucklers, the bows and the arrows, and the handstaves, and the spears, and they shall burn them with fire seven years. Ezekiel 39:9 KJV

Some think these Scriptures are referring to activity in Israel before or near the beginning of the Tribulation, but they are not. Israel will not be cleaning up the weapons of war during the seven years of the Tribulation. They will still be involved in military conflict until the end of Armageddon and they will be invaded and conquered three and a half years into the Tribulation. The seven years of peace and reclamation described here will not begin until Israel is finally dwelling in peace under Christ's rule.

Then, as the Scriptures tell us, once Jesus returns, in Israel alone, it is going to take the local population seven months to bury the dead and seven years to dispose of the weapons of war during the first part of the Millennium, and it is a pretty logical conclusion to say that the same thing will be happening around the rest of the World during the same time period.

While the remnant of humanity is involved in doing that

during the first part of the Millennium, God Himself will have removed the curse from nature and be restoring our planet back to a near-Eden state. Remember, God is not the killer in our present world system. God is good. He is the Giver of life. The Scriptures declare that Satan is the enemy who has the power of evil and death, and when he is gone, the curse of corruption and death will be lifted off nature, and things will return to the way they were when God first created them.

In that day the wolf and the lamb will live together; the leopard will lie down with the baby goat. The calf and the yearling will be safe with the lion, and a little child will lead them all. The cow will graze near the bear. The cub and the calf will lie down together. The lion will eat hay like a cow. The baby will play safely near the hole of a cobra. Yes, a little child will put its hand in a nest of deadly snakes without harm. Nothing will hurt or destroy in all my holy mountain, for as the waters fill the sea, so the earth will be filled with people who know the Lord. Isaiah 11:6-9 NLT

The wolf and the lamb will feed together. The lion will eat hay like a cow. But the snakes will eat dust. In those days no one will be hurt or destroyed on my holy mountain. I, the Lord, have spoken!" Isaiah 65:25 NLT

Yes, once the Millennium has begun, even human life spans will be greatly extended again. They will once again measured in centuries, not decades. Those mortals who choose to turn against God during the Millennium will still be subject to sickness and death due to God's judgement, and the evil consuming them, but for those who love God, this is what God promises us will happen:

No longer will babies die when only a few days old. No longer will adults die before they have lived a full life. No longer will people be considered old at one hundred! Only the cursed will die that young! Isaiah 65:20 NLT

You see, during the Millennium, the only place in all the Earth where the knowledge of evil will not yet be totally eradicated will be in the hearts and minds of the mortal (natural) men and women who repopulate the Earth during the Millennium. Even though these "elect" chose God during the Tribulation, they and their descendants will still have the sin nature within their mortal bodies, and that is going to create a problem during the Millennium.

They will still be capable of rebelling against God, still be corruptible, still be vulnerable to deception, and in the end, the Scriptures reveal to us that most will again side with Satan when he makes his last stand against Christ after he is released for a short season at the end of the Millennium. As to how and why this will all happen, that is part of a much larger discussion which (Lord willing) I will cover in my next book, "The Tribulation, the Millennium and Beyond"

Who is The Bride of Christ?

There are very few Scripture passages in the Bible where you will not be able to find someone somewhere who will disagree with you regarding what the passage means, and the identity of the Bride of Christ is no exception. There are those today who insist that the Bride of Christ can only be Israel. They teach that the five wise virgins in Christ's parable of the ten virgins are Israel and the five foolish ones are the rest of the world.

Others use the following Scriptures in Revelation to insist that the wise virgins in Matthew 25 are believers, but suggest that believers are only the bridesmaids, and the "bride" is the inanimate Heavenly Jerusalem which will come down from God after the Millennium when God burns up the existing universe, and creates a new Heavens and Earth:

Then I saw a new heaven and a new earth, for the old heaven and the old earth had disappeared. And the sea was also gone. And I saw the holy city, the new Jerusalem, coming down from God out of heaven like a bride beautifully dressed for her husband. Revelation 21:1-2 NLT

Then one of the seven angels who held the seven bowls containing the seven last plagues came and said to me, "Come with me! I will show you the bride, the wife of the Lamb." So he took me in the Spirit to a great, high mountain, and he showed me the holy city, Jerusalem, descending out of heaven from God. Revelation 21:9-10 NLT

What is happening in our generation is that (because some do not want to believe that the church is the bride) they are pointing to these Scriptures and arguing that it says here that the Heavenly Jerusalem, the buildings and the streets and the walls which will be coming down are Christ's bride, and really, that does not make any more sense than arguing that the building which Christians gather in on Earth today is the "church".

The only reason that we should ever be calling an Earthly building a "church" is because it **contains** the believers in God who ARE the church. Likewise, when the Heavenly Jerusalem descends from the Third Heaven to become the eternal capital city for humanity, the reason that it will be called the "bride" is because we who ARE the "bride" will be descending with the Holy City to reign and rule with Christ forever.

John the Baptist was the last of the Old Testament prophets, and one of the things that he understood was that all of the Old Testament believers were the "friends" of the groom, and so John was not upset when Jesus began to have more followers than he did or that some of his disciples were beginning to move over to follow Jesus. John understood that the people following him were not his to have. John was merely a friend of the groom, readying the virgins for the arrival of the Bridegroom.

John rejoiced that people were transitioning to Jesus because John knew that those who believed in Jesus were the ones who would become Christ's bride after He rose from the dead. Speaking of his own ministry, and that of Jesus Christ, John said:

He who has the bride is the bridegroom; but the friend of the bridegroom, who stands and hears him, rejoices greatly because of the bridegroom's voice. Therefore this joy of mine is fulfilled. John 3:29 NKJV

Therefore, we should understand that the reason the Heavenly Jerusalem is referred to as the "bride" is not because the buildings themselves are the bride any more than the buildings today containing the church are the church. If we go to 2 Corinthians, we see that the Apostle Paul gives a very clear picture of who the virgins are and who the Bride of Christ is:

> For I am jealous over you with godly jealousy: for I have espoused you to one husband, that I may present you as a chaste virgin to Christ. 2 Corinthians 11:2 KJV

Yes, dear reader. You and I are the wise virgins espoused to Christ, and we will be His Bride coming down from Heaven in the Heavenly Jerusalem. Christ can no more love and spiritually marry an inanimate city than we can. Love is something that beings have for one another. Consequently, we can know that the "bride" of Christ is not the Heavenly Jerusalem itself, but those who will be in God's Holy city, those who will be descending with it to reign and rule with Christ forever.

The same thing goes for Israel. When God says that He loves Jerusalem and Israel, He is not talking about the buildings which form Jerusalem or the cities which are in Israel. God is talking about the people of Israel. Beings love other beings, not inanimate objects.

Chapter 9

The Wrath of God

Is the Bride of Christ Appointed to Wrath?

Most of us have heard God say in His Word that the righteous are not appointed to wrath, but what does that mean? Does that mean that God's plan for the coming Tribulation is to protect existing Christians as we all go "through" the seven year tribulation? Is the truth, as some say, that only the last half of the Tribulation is God's wrath? Or does God's wrath start at the beginning of the Tribulation, (as pre-trib doctrine claims,) and continue to build and worsen for the entire seven years?

Hopefully, the previous chapters were helpful enough for the reader to comprehend that I believe that the Scriptures and the character of God indicate that a post-tribulation Rapture is not a realistic future for believers according to the Bible. Remember, God says there will be no one else left living to be raptured at the end of the Tribulation if the wicked are destroyed and the believers are going into the Millennium in their natural bodies to repopulate the Earth during those thousand years.

Yet there is more to it than that. The other reason I believe that the Bride of Christ will not be going through the Tribulation is that the Word of God repeatedly points out to us that God's wrath is intended for the wicked, not for those who love and follow Him. Christ's wrath is not for his Bride made righteous by our faith in Jesus Christ.

Therefore, the worldwide corporate church (God's spiritual nation which came into being when the nation of Israel was cut off because of their unbelief) is NOT appointed to endure this coming time of wrath that will befall this unrepentant, wicked and adulterous generation of humanity:

But God demonstrates His own love toward us, in that while we were still sinners, Christ died for us. Much more then, having now been justified by His blood, we shall be saved from wrath through Him. Romans 5:8-9 NKJV

For God did not appoint us to wrath, but to obtain salvation through our Lord Jesus Christ, who died for us, that whether we wake or sleep, we should live together with Him. Therefore comfort each other and edify one another, just as you also are doing. 1 Thessalonians 5:9-11 NKJV

I assure you that it is not very comforting or edifying, neither does it inspire hope in people when preachers and teachers ignore and contradict what God says here because they have some sort of martyr complex and are convinced that we will not be saved "from" the wrath of God through our faith in God.

On the contrary, they are teaching that all believers will

be required to go "through" the coming wrath of God as a kind of "torture test" of our faith. Yet, does the Bible teach that this is the real purpose of the Tribulation? Is the purpose of the Tribulation to try or "test" our faith?

Often, the teachers of a post-tribulation rapture will counter what I just said by quoting Scriptures listing how God did not remove Daniel, but protected him in the lion's den. Likewise, they will say that God required Shadrach, Meshach and Abednego to go through the fiery furnace and God protected them in the midst of tribulation. They also point out that God protected Moses and Israel, but they still had to go "through" the Red Sea.

The problem with all these examples is that the people who use them totally ignore the Biblical context in which they occurred. Not one of these miracles would have been necessary if the nation of Israel had listened to God and remained faithful to the instructions Abraham (and later Moses) had given them from God.

As far as the bunch who were with Moses goes, they are not a very good example or shadow of the Bride of Christ. Yes, the nation of Israel was rescued by God from Egypt, but, with the exception of Joshua and Caleb, NONE of them made it to the Promised Land. They all died in the wilderness due to their repeated living in unbelief and walking in evil ways.

So, rather than being a good example of a "type" of the Bride of Christ, historical Israel is a much closer example or shadow of the unrepentant who will miss the Rapture, and even if they do repent later, will still almost all die during the Tribulation:

That is why the Holy Spirit says, "Today when you hear his voice, don't harden your hearts as Israel did when they rebelled, when they tested me in the wilderness. There your ancestors tested and tried my patience, even though they saw my miracles for forty years. So I was angry with them, and I said 'Their hearts always turn away from me. They refuse to do what I tell them.' So in my anger I took an oath: 'They will never enter my place of rest.'" Hebrews 3:7-11 NLT

The often quoted Scriptures as proof that the Bride of Christ will go through the tribulation are actually all examples God's protection of the righteous from the perspective of Israel as a nation being ALREADY in the midst of tribulation because they had repeatedly been disobedient, unrepentant and following the Devil instead of God. Yet, God still had mercy and helped some who remained faithful during the years that the nation of Israel was in repeated tribulation due to their sin.

So, these examples are not at all an indication of God's desire for the Bride to go through the Tribulation, but a glimmer of hope for those who come to Christ DURING the Tribulation that, even after the Bride is gone and the door to Heaven has been closed again, with God's help they can still be saved, and there is a slim hope that they might be one of those who survive to the end. If you want to know the closest "shadow" of what the Rapture is going to be like, instead look at the life of Enoch:

After the birth of Methuselah, Enoch lived in close fellowship with God for another 300 years, and he had other sons and daughters. Enoch lived 365 years, walking in close fellowship with God. Then one day he disappeared, because God took him. Genesis 5:22-24 NLT

There are quite a few other examples which post-tribulation teachers use to support their ideas, but the most prominent one is their insistence that God did not completely remove Noah from the Earth. Therefore, they teach that since God did not remove Noah and his family "from" the judgement of God, but protected them as they went "through" it, and they say the same thing will happen again when the Tribulation begins.

How then do we reconcile this with God's declarations that the righteous are not appointed to wrath? Wait a minute! First of all, God did not put Noah and his family "through" the wrath. God Himself closed Noah and his family in a giant Ark, shutting them in so they could not even see what was going on outside, and floating them high above God's wrathful cleansing of the Earth. Compare this to the terrifying future that awaits people during the Tribulation according to God's description of the death and destruction that will be happening in full view of everyone as they go through the Tribulation.

If there is no Rapture of the living until the end of the Tribulation, the beloved Bride of Christ would be totally immersed in the middle of the worst holocaust in human history (worse than what happened to the Jews in WWII.)

Every Christian would be going through the traumatic experience of watching billions and billions of people dying all around us for seven long years, including many friends and family, and almost none of us surviving until Christ returns during Armageddon to put an end to humanity's madness before ALL flesh is completely destroyed. Does this sound like a future planned for us by a loving God who has appointed His Son's beloved to receive mercy, not wrath?

You see, no matter how much tribulation and persecution increases in Canada and the U.S. before the Tribulation, this is still not the WRATH of God. The common element in the wrath of God throughout the Bible is that, when it happens, ALMOST EVERYBODY DIES. That's what happened in Noah's day. That's what happened in Sodom, and that is what is going to happen once again during the coming Tribulation. The backslidden professing Christians of this present generation need to learn the lesson from what happened when Israel refused to listen to Moses, and repeatedly turned back to disobedience and sin during their deliverance from Egypt. The wrath of God was finally kindled against them and ALMOST EVERYONE DIED, with only Joshua and Caleb of that generation being able to enter the Promised Land in their natural lifetime.

"Do not harden your hearts, as in the rebellion, as in the day of trial in the wilderness, when your fathers tested Me. They tried Me, though they saw My work. For forty years I was grieved with that generation, and said, 'It is a people who go astray in their hearts, and they do not know My ways.' So I swore in My wrath, 'They shall not enter My rest.' " Psalm 95:8-11 KJV

For then there will be great tribulation, such as has not been since the beginning of the world until this time, no, nor ever shall be. And unless those days were shortened, no flesh would be saved; but for the elect's sake those days will be shortened. Matthew 24:21-22 NKJV

What is the Real Purpose of the Tribulation?

Is the purpose of God's wrath that the coming Tribulation will be His "torture test" for the Bride of Christ so we can suffer for seven years to prove ourselves worthy to be wedded to Jesus and receive eternal life after we are raptured? Let's take a look at what the Scriptures say about the wrath of God:

For see, the day of the Lord is coming— the terrible day of his fury and fierce anger. The land will be made desolate, and all the sinners destroyed with it.Isaiah 13:9 NLT

I, the Lord, will punish the world for its evil and the wicked for their sin. I will crush the arrogance of the proud and humble the pride of the mighty. I will make people scarcer than gold—more rare than the fine gold of Ophir. For I will shake the heavens. The earth will move from its place when the Lord of Heaven's Armies displays his wrath in the day of his fierce anger. Isaiah 13:11-13 NLT

To me, this looks very much like God's purpose for his wrath is not to torture the righteous, but to punish and crush the arrogance of the wicked to bring them to a place of repentance. So, what else does God's Word have to say to us about His wrath?

He who believes in the Son has everlasting life; and he who does not believe the Son shall not see life, but the wrath of God abides on him." John 3:36 NKJV

For the wrath of God is revealed from heaven against all ungodliness and unrighteousness of men, who suppress the truth in unrighteousness. Romans 1:18 NKJV

But because you are stubborn and refuse to turn from your sin, you are storing up terrible punishment for yourself. For a day of anger is coming, when God's righteous judgment will be revealed. He will judge everyone according to what they have done. He will give eternal life to those who keep on doing good, seeking after the glory and honor and immortality that God offers. But he will pour out his anger and wrath on those who live for themselves, who refuse to obey the truth and instead live lives of wickedness. There will be trouble and calamity for everyone who keeps on doing what is evil—for the Jew first and also for the Gentile. Romans 2:5-9 NLT

I do not think that this is very hard to understand or that there can be any confusion here. God does test our faith at times during our lives, but He says in His Word that the purpose of His WRATH is to deal with the wicked, not test the righteous:

But fornication and all uncleanness or covetousness, let it not even be named among you, as is fitting for saints; neither filthiness, nor foolish talking, nor coarse jesting, which are not fitting, but rather giving of thanks. For this you know, that no fornicator, unclean person, nor covetous man, who is an idolater, has any inheritance in the kingdom of Christ and God. Let no one deceive you with empty words, for because of these things the wrath of God comes upon the sons of disobedience. Therefore do not be partakers with them. Ephesians 5:3-7 NKJV

So put to death the sinful, earthly things lurking within you. Have nothing to do with sexual immorality, impurity, lust, and evil desires. Don't be greedy, for a greedy person is an idolater, worshiping the things of this world. Because of these sins, the anger of God is coming. Colossians 3:5-7 NLT

I think we have a pretty clear picture here that God is warning us to depart from evil because it is not God's will for us to experience any of God's wrath, but that His wrath will come upon the unrighteous and the disobedient in these last days. In the NKJV, Colossians says here that, "because of these things the wrath of God is coming upon the sons of disobedience." This now brings us to the question of WHEN the wrath of God will actually begin, if it is not going to happen at the beginning of the Tribulation.

Mid Tribulation Rapture?

There are more than a few professing Christians today who are preaching and teaching that the Resurrection of deceased believers and the Rapture of living believers is not actually going to happen until close to the middle of the

Tribulation, and they too offer a few Scriptures to support their point of view.

The basic premise of the mid-trib belief is that (like pre-tribulation believers) they also do not believe that God wants, or is going to require, the Bride of Christ to endure God's wrath. However, those who teach a mid-tribulation Rapture are convinced that the "wrath" of God will not begin until approximately the middle of the Tribulation.

They suggest that all of the problems which will occur during the first half of the Tribulation are going to be the results of the wrath of man and the wrath of Satan, not the wrath of God.

This version of a mid-trib Rapture is also sometimes referred to as the "pre-wrath" Rapture doctrine. An important aspect of the teaching of a mid-tribulation rapture is that they believe there will be a time of relative "false" peace during the first part of the Tribulation when the Antichrist begins to rise to power.

They teach that the Antichrist will utilize his charisma, diplomacy, and deception (with the support of the False Prophet) to deceive the world and ascend to the position of world leader during the first half of the Tribulation, with little bloodshed at first. They insist that the wrath of God will not actually begin until after the breaking of the sixth seal in Revelation 6.

Then everyone—the kings of the earth, the rulers, the generals, the wealthy, the powerful, and every slave and free person—all hid themselves in the caves and among the rocks of the mountains. And they cried to the mountains and the rocks, "Fall on us and hide us from the face of the one who sits on the throne and from the wrath of the Lamb. For the great day of their wrath has come, and who is able to survive?" Revelation 6:15-17 NLT

However, it is not a universal position among mid-trib believers that the wrath of God begins that close to the beginning of the Tribulation. There are also other mid-tribulation teachers who suggest that the Rapture will not occur until considerably later than that.

From their perspective, they teach that the Rapture will occur just before the Antichrist double-crosses Israel and stands in their temple proclaiming himself to be God and demanding that he be worshipped as God, and anyone who does not worship him as God will be killed. Since God says in his Word that this political scenario will not come to pass until three and a half years into the Tribulation, the term "mid-tribulation" is thus quite accurate for the idea that the rapture will occur at this particular time.

The 70ᵗʰ Week of Daniel

The coming seven year Great Tribulation period is also referred to in Scripture as the seventieth, or last, week of Daniel, speaking of a week of years = seven years. We can also glean from the book of Daniel that during this last seven years of Satan's rule over humanity, at the beginning of the Tribulation, the Antichrist is going to broker and enforce a seven year peace treaty between Israel and all of her enemies.

Although the language is still a bit archaic, even in most modern translations, what we learn from Daniel 9:25-

27 is that while Daniel is praying and pleading to God for Jerusalem, the Angel Gabriel comes to Daniel in a vision. Gabriel reveals to Daniel that there would be a period of exactly 483 years (7 sets of 7 years plus 62 sets of seven years) that would pass from the time that the command went out to rebuild the temple in Jerusalem until the time the Messiah would be slain in Israel, and that prophecy came to pass in history EXACTLY as Daniel said it would.

Gabriel then said that shortly after that, the Jerusalem temple which existed in Christ's day would be destroyed and another one would not be rebuilt until "the end," and that particular prophecy of the destruction of the Temple in Jerusalem would also come to pass in 70 A.D., just as the angel Gabriel said it would. The Temple in Jerusalem has not been rebuilt since, but it will be soon. Then Daniel tells us that the last thing Gabriel said to him was an event would occur at the very end of the last days:

The ruler will make a treaty with the people for a period of one set of seven, but after half this time, he will put an end to the sacrifices and offerings. And as a climax to all his terrible deeds, he will set up a sacrilegious object that causes desecration, until the fate decreed for this defiler is finally poured out on him." Daniel 9:27 NLT

So, the Antichrist is going to orchestrate a seven year peace treaty protecting Israel. This treaty is also confirmed in several places in the book of Revelation, where God declares that the Antichrist will rule the world virtually undefeatable for the first half of the Tribulation and the city of Jerusalem will still be trodden down by Gentiles because Israel will still be blinded in unbelief, not yet having come to Christ as a nation.

Yet, God will allow Israel's Temple to be rebuilt in Jerusalem, and this will result in a zealous resurgence of Judaism, with Israel in their unhealed spiritual blindness trying to please God while continuing to reject Jesus Christ as the Messiah and Savior of the World.

And there was given unto him a mouth speaking great things and blasphemies; and power was given unto him to continue forty and two months. And he opened his mouth in blasphemy against God, to blaspheme his name, and his tabernacle, and them that dwell in heaven. And it was given unto him to make war with the saints, and to overcome them: and power was given him over all kindreds, and tongues, and nations. Revelation 13:5-7 KJV

Here, we find that during the first half of the seven year tribulation, ALL, the whole world, will eventually come under Antichrist's control, and they will submit to him, including Israel. During this time, the Temple itself in Israel and their religious liberty will be under the protection of the Antichrist during the first half of the Tribulation (42 months, or 1260 days).

However, because Israel as a nation will still be rejecting Christ during this time, their Temple, their religious services, and all of their sacrifices will not be pleasing to the Lord. Furthermore, the whole world will be outraged when Israel begins to institute daily sacrificing of thousands of animals to God in their temple. The whole world will be enraged about it, and the animal rights activism that is now gaining momentum all around the world is going to place tremendous pressure on the Antichrist to demand Israel cease these sacrifices.

Of course, Israel will not do this because (in their continuing spiritual blindness of rejecting Christ) they will still think they are doing service to God and pleasing God with their Old Testament rituals. So, half-way through the Tribulation (after 1260 days or about three and a half years, according to the Jewish calendar) God will allow the Antichrist to invade and conquer Israel, put an end to the sacrifices, and take over the Temple in Jerusalem, declaring that he is God over all people and demanding that the whole world worship him or die.

> Then I was given a measuring stick, and I was told, "Go and measure the Temple of God and the altar, and count the number of worshipers. But do not measure the outer courtyard, for it has been turned over to the nations. They will trample the holy city for 42 months. And I will give power to my two witnesses, and they will be clothed in burlap and will prophesy during those 1,260 days." Revelation 11:1-3 NLT

> When they complete their testimony, the beast that comes up out of the bottomless pit will declare war against them, and he will conquer them and kill them. Revelation 11:7 NLT

Here we see that, in spite of the false religion going on in Israel during the first half of the Tribulation, God will also have two prophets or witnesses of Christ who will preach the truth from Jerusalem during those first three and a half years until the Antichrist kills them when He invades Israel.

This murder of God's prophets, the desecration of Israel's temple, and the Antichrist's blasphemous claim to be God will (of course) be the foolish act that God will use to turn the world against the Antichrist and the backbench scheming, which will have been going on since the beginning of the Tribulation, will finally break out into full-scale world war Armageddon (WWIII,) which will destroy almost all flesh on Earth during the second half of the Tribulation.

When does the Wrath of God Begin?

The whole premise of the pre-wrath or mid-tribulation teaching is that they (like pre-tribbers) do not believe the Bride of Christ is appointed to wrath, but the mid-tribbers have developed the idea in their minds that the first half of the Tribulation will be relatively peaceful while the Antichrist rises to power, almost entirely as a result of his demonically supernatural charisma, his political scheming and lying, and this will mean that there will be at least a semblance of worldwide peace for a while.

Their contention is that any "wrath" that happens during the first half of the Tribulation is merely the wrath of man and the wrath of Satan, suggesting that the wrath of God does not begin until mid-tribulation.

They are thus relying on believers having plenty of time to take their guns and supplies and head for their underground bunkers or caves in the wilderness when they see the Antichrist begin to rise to power because things are not going to be so bad for the first three and a half years, but again, is that really what the Word of God teaches?

In my opinion, these people have formulated some seriously mistaken conclusions based on very flimsy Scriptural evidence. To begin with, military technology is still advancing at a phenomenal rate. If they had the technology ten years ago to find Osama Bin Laden in a cave in the mountains, unless God helps hide you, they are certainly going to find you during the Tribulation if they want to.

Yes, God tells us that, for the purpose of the survival of the elect, God will still offer a measure of protection over a few during the Tribulation. However, if the pre-tribulation rapture does happen, those who are left behind should be wise and immediately take off for the hardships of the wilderness where they need to spend their time coming back to God and following in His ways.

If there is a pre-tribulation Rapture, it will be extremely important for the people who are left behind to prepare their hearts for what will be coming, beginning to comprehend that if they survive the coming holocaust, it will not be as the result of their bunkers, or rations, or weapons, or any of their own ability to defend themselves, but because God in His grace will help those who turn to Him for mercy.

That brings us to what the Bible actually says is going to happen during the first half of the Tribulation and how bad it is going to get for the people who are on Earth during that terrible time.

And there appeared a great wonder in heaven; a woman clothed with the sun, and the moon under her feet, and upon her head a crown of twelve stars...And she brought forth a man child, who was to rule all nations with a rod of iron: and her child was caught up unto God, and to his throne. Revelation 12:1, 5 KJV

Let's start with the nation of Israel. In Revelation 12, God talks about the woman (true Israel) who brings forth the man child (Jesus) who is caught up to Heaven. Some suggest that this Scripture is referring to the whole nation of Israel and Jesus alone, but there is more to it than that. It was not the entire nation of Israel who brought forth the man child in Israel. It was the true children of Abraham, and these same true children of Abraham were the founders of the church with the help and power of the Holy Spirit. Therefore, here "the woman" is referring to all true believers, both Jews and Gentiles.

The man child here refers to both Jesus (the Head of the church) and the church (His body) being caught up to God. Later on, when the Antichrist invades Israel half way through the Tribulation, the context of the Scripture describing that event indicates that the "woman" in that passage is referring specifically to believers in Israel (almost exclusively Jews) who will need to flee or die. Yet, at this point in Revelation 12:6, the "woman" still represents a large segment of humanity who will flee to the wilderness and seek God (both Jew and Gentile) during the first half of the Tribulation.

And the woman fled into the wilderness, where she hath a place prepared of God, that they should feed her there a thousand two hundred and threescore days. Revelation 12:6 KJV

God specifically warns believers here who come to Christ during the first half of the Tribulation to flee to the wilderness. Why? There is going to be immediate worldwide persecution of Christians right after the Rapture, right at the beginning of the Tribulation. Even with the 144,000 and the two witnesses preaching, the resurgence of Judaism in Israel means that Christians will come under intense persecution there, and the same thing is going to happen throughout the world as the False Prophet and the Antichrist are able to quickly deceive the whole world into ostracizing Bible-believing Christians as "anti-society".

Is there any real Biblical support for the idea that the wrath of God does not begin until the second half of the Tribulation? Let's take a look at their argument that God's wrath does not start until the opening of the sixth seal in the book of Revelation. I think you will find that, contrary to what is being taught in mid-tribulation circles, God's Word says that the Antichrist's rise to power is not at all going to be a peaceful transition. It will be bloody and deadly right from the beginning.

And I beheld when he had opened the sixth seal, and, lo, there was a great earthquake; and the sun became black as sackcloth of hair, and the moon became as blood; and the stars of heaven fell unto the earth, even as a fig tree casteth her untimely figs, when she is shaken of a mighty wind. And the heaven departed as a scroll when it is rolled together; and every mountain and island were moved out of their places.

And the kings of the earth, and the great men, and the rich men, and the chief captains, and the mighty men, and every bondman, and every free man, hid themselves in the dens and in the rocks of the mountains; And said to the mountains and rocks, Fall on us, and hide us from the face of him that sitteth on the throne, and from the wrath of the Lamb: For the great day of his wrath is come; and who shall be able to stand? Revelation 6:12-17 KJV

The argument used by mid-trib believers is that, because the wrath of God is not mentioned until this point in the book of Revelation, this means that it is not happening yet, and will begin with the opening of the sixth seal, but that is because they are displaying a basic lack of understanding of the English that was used at the time the KJV was written and the Greek that was used to produce the KJV in the first place, not to mention ignoring the whole context of the passage.

To begin with, the usage of the phrase "day of his wrath" here in the context that is given is not referring to a twenty-four hour period, but an indistinct time period, just as it does in many other places throughout Scripture, or if one would say "in my day, we did not do this." More importantly though, we need to take a look at the phrase "is come". The phrase does not mean that God's wrath is coming afterward, but rather, it is stating that his wrath is already here.

It would be just as accurate to translate this passage as "the great time of God's wrath is here," and you will hopefully see that when you realize all of the tremendous carnage that will have already occurred from the time the Tribulation begins, and continuing until this opening of the sixth seal.

As we look a little further back in Revelation 6, it becomes clear that, before this sixth seal is even opened, there will literally be billions of people who will enter the Tribulation alive and already be dead from various causes before the opening of the sixth seal.

It is also important for the reader to realize that the opening of the sixth seal is an event which happens very near the BEGINNING of the Tribulation (not at the middle) which does not really support a mid-tribulation rapture if the rapture occurs just before the opening of the sixth seal.

There are some who argue that the different Judgements of God will happen concurrently, meaning that the trumpet Judgements will happen at the same time as the seal Judgements and therefore the sixth seal Judgement does come at the middle of the Tribulation.

However, there is nothing at all in the context of the Book of Revelation to suggest that the judgements of God during the Tribulation will happen this way. They will occur consecutively (one after the other) in increasing severity with each round of Judgements.

So, first there is the seal judgements, then the trumpet Judgements, followed by the bowl Judgements, and the middle of the Tribulation does not arrive until after the sixth trumpet Judgement when the Antichrist double crosses and invades Israel exactly three and a half years into the Tribulation.

Chapter 10

The Tribulation Begins

The Opening of the Seal Judgements

Since the study of the Book of Revelation and the seven year Tribulation is almost a book in itself, we are not going to cover the whole Tribulation period here, but I believe that it is important for us to take a look at some of the judgements of God which occur at the beginning of the Tribulation and how they line up with the idea of there being no wrath of God until a mid-tribulation rapture.

For the purpose of examining the claims of those who promote the idea of a mid-tribulation rapture, let's take a close look at the first two judgements of God, the seal judgements and the trumpet judgements.

For a more thorough examination of the Tribulation and Millennium (which the Bible declares is going to be considerably different from many of the concepts that are being taught from some pulpits today,) keep watching for my newest book "THE TRIBULATION, THE MILLENNIUM, AND BEYOND" which I am now working on and hope to be able to have in print later this year, Lord willing.

Let us begin by going over the first judgement of God, which the Lord declares will occur right at the beginning of the Tribulation, referred to as the 1st seal judgement, the arrival of the rider on the white horse:

And I saw when the Lamb opened one of the seals, and I heard, as it were the noise of thunder, one of the four beasts saying, "Come and see". And I saw, and behold a white horse: and he that sat on him had a bow; and a crown was given unto him: and he went forth conquering, and to conquer. Revelation 6:1-2 KJV

Now, one of the things that is so important when we are studying the Bible is CONTEXT. How does the verse or portion of the verse fit with the rest of the inspired Scripture surrounding it? There are professing Christians running around in these last days trying to say that the rider on the white horse is Jesus, "because the good guys always ride a white horse." These people have been watching too much TV and are leading people astray.

Look carefully at the passage. Jesus (the Lamb) is in the Third Heaven opening the seal. The rider on the white horse is on Earth about to cause carnage. The symbolism of the white horse suggests that the rider is going to go forth "proclaiming" love, goodness, world peace and all of the other things that our current world leaders are already promising if we follow them. This rider on the white horse will be the Antichrist, and although one of the main components of his political platform will be the promise of world peace, the prophet Daniel warns us:

And through his policy also he shall cause craft to prosper in his hand; and he shall magnify himself in his heart, and by peace shall destroy many: he shall also stand up against the Prince of princes; but he shall be broken without hand. Daniel 8:25 KJV

What Daniel and the book of Revelation are saying here is that through the Antichrist's slippery politics and "craft" (deception and witchcraft, really), and with the promise of peace, the Antichrist is going to begin his rise to power by conquering nations, and it is important to understand that his agenda will be to continue to conquer, keep conquering, just like Hitler did in WWII.

Antichrist on the White Horse

Those who really want to believe there to be little or no bloodshed during the first half of the Tribulation have emphasized that there is no mention of arrows in Revelation's description of the rider on the white horse wielding a bow when he goes forth to conquer.

They say this suggests that the Antichrist will not use military force during his rise to world dominance during the first half of the Tribulation. Rather, he will use his satanic charisma, the political power of his ten nation alliance, and the "threat" of military force to convince the whole world to follow him.

It all sounds nice, but the "no arrow" argument is a pretty flimsy conclusion based solely upon the fact that arrows are not mentioned here when the Antichrist goes out to conquer. In that time in history, the bow was the choice of almost every nation for long distance combat. The white horse is definitely in line with a political platform promising world peace, but the Scriptures are pretty clear here that the Antichrist will use military campaigns to conquer nations and enforce his "peace."

There is no need for John to mention arrows in Revelation any more than there would be to mention bullets in guns or shells in the tanks and cannons of any modern army because no one would go into a battle with a weapon and no ammunition.

Furthermore, when the armies advanced on an enemy in Biblical times, the archers were the first line of attack. They performed the "first strike" from a distance, and then when their enemy was weakened, the foot soldiers would move in and finish them off at close quarters.

This idea of "no significant military force" being prominent during the first half of the Tribulation also doesn't line up at all with what happens when the very next seal is broken in Heaven and the rider on the red horse goes forth. God tells us that peace will be taken from the Earth and war will break out. Let's take a look at that now.

Initial Opposition to Antichrist

No! The whole world is not going to immediately fall in behind the Antichrist and his ten nation alliance right from the beginning. Yes, the Antichrist is going to rise to power on a political platform promising world peace and prosperity. However, when he goes forth to begin conquering and enforcing his dominion over all nations, there WILL be some resistance that will have to be put down militarily, and that resistance will break out in war almost right from the very beginning of the Tribulation:

And when he had opened the second seal, I heard the second beast say, Come and see. And there went out another horse that was red: and power was given to him that sat thereon to take peace from the earth, and that they should kill one another: and there was given unto him a great sword. Revelation 6:3-4 KJV

What we see here is that, contrary to what mid-tribulationists are teaching, even though the Antichrist will be promising peace, and he brokers and enforces a seven year treaty protecting Israel, there will be no world peace in general. Very shortly after the Tribulation begins, war will break out between the Antichrist's forces and those nations who oppose him, and things are going to get very bad and very bloody on Earth, very quickly.

The sheer ruthlessness and overwhelming force that the Antichrist's forces will inflict on all who come against him at the beginning of the Tribulation will quickly put the world into such a state of fear that most of the world will soon bow to his rule, but there will be tremendous collateral damage as a result of these initial wars.

And when he had opened the third seal, I heard the third beast say, Come and see. And I beheld, and lo a black horse;

and he that sat on him had a pair of balances in his hand. And I heard a voice in the midst of the four beasts say, 'A measure of wheat for a penny, and three measures of barley for a penny; and see thou hurt not the oil and the wine.' Revelation 6:5-6 KJV

What we see here is a very clear picture of the fallout (collateral damage) from the military conflicts between the Antichrist and those who oppose him. This will bring on a worldwide economic depression and lack of food, and be quickly followed by starvation, famine and a great increase in animal predation of human beings because, obviously, many animals will also be starving due to the lack of food in general.

And when he had opened the fourth seal, I heard the voice of the fourth beast say, "Come and see". And I looked, and behold a pale horse: and his name that sat on him was Death, and Hell followed with him. And power was given unto them over the fourth part of the earth, to kill with sword, and with hunger, and with death, and with the beasts of the earth. Revelation 6:7-8 KJV

Just in case you missed it, God is telling us here that **one quarter** of the human population is going to die in this one judgement, this one military conflict alone. If there is no Rapture before this point in the future, (as the mid-trib teachers claim) this means that approximately two billion people will die during the second seal judgement, right after the beginning of the tribulation.

Mid-tribulation advocates tend to dispute this high death

toll by arguing that the passage does not actually say that one-quarter of the POPULATION will die, only that death and hell will be given power over one-quarter of the Earth.

What? Do you think that this means that death and hell will only affect sparsely populated areas where people will die and the number will probably be far less? That is highly unlikely in a time of war. On the contrary, during war, it is usually the more populated areas that suffer.

What if the one quarter of the Earth that is affected is the Middle East and China? If that is the case, we are talking about half the human population instead of one quarter. Two billion deaths during this fourth seal judgement at the beginning of the Tribulation is (if anything) a conservative estimate of how horrible it will be during the beginning of the Tribulation. Yet that will not be all that will be going on during this time:

And when he had opened the fifth seal, I saw under the altar the souls of them that were slain for the word of God, and for the testimony which they held: And they cried with a loud voice, saying, How long, O Lord, holy and true, dost thou not judge and avenge our blood on them that dwell on the earth? And white robes were given unto every one of them; and it was said unto them, that they should rest yet for a little season, until their fellow servants also and their brethren, that should be killed as they were, should be fulfilled. Revelation 6:9-11 KJV

Regardless of when you believe the Rapture will be occurring, here again we have evidence that the first half of the Tribulation is not going to be any relatively peaceful time for those who already profess to be Christian and those who come to Christ during the first half of the Tribulation.

Actually, I believe the Scriptures indicate that the pre-millennial Rapture is going to trigger a huge number of conversions to Jesus Christ. There will be a massive revival of Christianity in the beginning, perhaps the largest in history, and the Antichrist is going to want to stamp that out right away.

Right from the beginning, Christians will be targeted by the Antichrist and the False Prophet as being disruptive and "anti-society." I will emphasize here that one of the things that pre-tribulation teachers firmly believe is taught in the Bible is that (after the Rapture) during Tribulation, people will still be able to be saved, but the Holy Spirit will not be present on the Earth restraining evil to the same extent that He is now, and that is HOW evil is able to escalate so swiftly and exponentially during those last seven years.

We believe the Scriptures indicate that when the Bride of Christ ascends to be with Jesus, the Holy Spirit residing in every believer will be going with us. After that, the relationship between the Holy Spirit and the remainder of humanity will revert to the way it was in the Old Testament.

Those who truly seek the Holy Spirit during the Tribulation will be able to access Him, as could Old Testament believers, but most of humanity will be led by the Devil during the Tribulation. Furthermore, many will be possessed by the multitudes of demons that will soon be cast out of their present dwelling place in the Second Heaven and confined to spending the last seven years of their existence on Earth.

These devils will all be confined to dwelling in the First Heaven immediately surrounding Earth and desiring to be inside the many who will open themselves up to demon possession during that time, and they will all hate Christians.

For the mystery of iniquity doth already work: only he who now letteth will let, until he be taken out of the way. And then shall that Wicked be revealed, whom the Lord shall consume with the spirit of his mouth, and shall destroy with the brightness of his coming: Even him, whose coming is after the working of Satan with all power and signs and lying wonders, And with all deceivableness of unrighteousness in them that perish; because they received not the love of the truth, that they might be saved. And for this cause God shall send them strong delusion, that they should believe a lie: That they all might be damned who believed not the truth, but had pleasure in unrighteousness. 2 Thessalonians 2:7-12 KJV

Since the language of the KJV is pretty awkward here, we can more easily see what Paul was saying in verse 7 by putting this verse in more modern language and paraphrase it as:

For the mystery of evil (sin) is already working, but the One who is restraining evil (the Holy Spirit within the body of Christ) will continue to do so until He is taken out of the way (when the Rapture occurs) 2 Thessalonians 2:7 (paraphrased)

Consequently, without the restraining force of Christians indwelt by the Holy Spirit's presence and power hindering evil, things are going to be bad, right from the beginning.

Already, during the recent Covid 19 scare, we have seen how quickly the government can take over and monopolize the television and the internet to preach their message and control the population.

Immediately after the Rapture, the Antichrist will be extremely successful using "anti-Christ" propaganda to lead the world into the delusion of believing that Biblical Christianity is evil. He will probably even be able to convince most of the world that Christians were responsible in an evil way for the disappearance of all those people.

The Antichrist's propaganda machine will likely refer to the disappearance of multitudes of people as an "abduction" rather than a Rapture, implicating Christians and convincing society to hate, persecute and kill real Christians everywhere right from the beginning.

Yet, false religion will continue to prosper under the leadership of the False Prophet, that is, until the Antichrist and False Prophet later on demand that the whole world must bow to the Antichrist and worship him only as God, or die.

The Opening of The 6ᵗʰ Seal

Remember now, at this point in the book of Revelation, mankind will still be right at the very beginning of the Tribulation period. Billions of people have already died worldwide during the first five seal judgements because of starvation, animal predation, persecution and war, and then Satan is going to top that off by bringing an unprecedented ecological disaster upon the very planet itself. It will be the worst environmental catastrophe that modern man has ever seen up to that point in human history

I watched as the Lamb broke the sixth seal, and there was a great earthquake. The sun became as dark as black cloth, and the moon became as red as blood. Then the stars of the sky fell to the earth like green figs falling from a tree shaken by a strong wind. The sky was rolled up like a scroll, and all of the mountains and islands were moved from their places. Revelation 6:12-14 NLT

Once a person really thinks a little about the magnitude of the disaster God is describing here, it does not take long to realize that this is no ordinary bout of bad weather or some natural disaster that humanity is already used to seeing. There will be a colossal earthquake, apparently accompanied by a volcanic eruption. The eruption will be so huge, and the sun will become so obscured, that it will seem as though there is a black cloth in front of it, and at night the moon will be so overcast that it will look like blood.

Then, right after that, there will be a quantity of "stars" which will punch through the Earth's Atmosphere and strike the Earth's crust with such force that it will flatten mountains and cause islands to disappear into the ocean.

Exactly what are these "stars" that God is speaking about? Since the Apostle John had never seen, or even imagined the idea of thermonuclear bombs when he wrote this passage, some have speculated that this could be nuclear missiles re-entering the atmosphere and exploding. Others have suggested that the "stars" will be a large meteor strike, which scientists have repeatedly predicted could happen in the near future.

For the point of this discussion, there is no purpose in haggling over which one it will be. The far more important issue is the worldwide devastation that this event will cause. The combined total of the immediate deaths as a result of the bombing of Hiroshima and Nagasaki was only about 100,000 people. The raining down of nuclear warheads much larger than those, or multiple meteors striking the Earth with the force of nuclear bombs combined with an earthquake and volcanic eruption so large that it flattens mountains and sinks islands will certainly result in many more deaths than this, perhaps into the millions, worldwide.

Are you beginning to see that the argument of mid-tribulation teachers that the first half of the Tribulation is going to be relatively peaceful, not so bad for Christians, perhaps only the wrath of man or the wrath of Satan, but certainly not the wrath of God, is not a realistic or Biblical portrayal of the way things are going to be for those remaining on Earth even during the BEGINNING of the first half of the Tribulation.

No! What we have just read is what it will really be like for humanity during the beginning of the first half of the Tribulation, and I do not at all believe that Father God has appointed Christ's Bride to endure this kind of wrath that God has already told us will be reserved for the wicked, not those who are made righteous in Christ:

Then everyone—the kings of the earth, the rulers, the generals, the wealthy, the powerful, and every slave and free person—all hid themselves in the caves and among the rocks of the mountains. And they cried to the mountains and the rocks, "Fall on us and hide us from the face of the one who sits on the throne and from the wrath of the Lamb. For the great day of their wrath has come, and who is able to survive?" Revelation 6:15-17 NLT

As I said before, this Scripture is not referring to God's wrath coming from then on. It is making it clear that by the time the Tribulation begins, God's wrath is already there. It has already come. Billions of people will already be dead by then, and many millions more will be dying all the time before the first trumpet Judgements even begin, still well within the first half of the Tribulation.

The Trumpet Judgements

Now, we are not going to take the space to record all of the trumpet judgements here. I encourage the reader to continue to slowly and carefully study the next judgements of God on your own (the trumpet judgements in Revelation 8 and 9.) These will all also occur during the first half of the Tribulation, still considerably BEFORE the Antichrist invades Israel mid-tribulation.

As you are reading in Revelation 8 and 9, add up the possible numbers of deaths from each trumpet judgement individually, paying particular attention to Revelation 9:15-18 which clearly states that as a result of the sixth judgement alone, one-third of the human population will die. For the sake of proving our point, let's at least look at the sixth trumpet judgement here

Then the four angels who had been prepared for this hour and day and month and year were turned loose to kill one-third of all the people on earth. I heard the size of their army, which was 200 million mounted troops. And in my vision, I saw the horses and the riders sitting on them. The riders wore armor that was fiery red and dark blue and yellow. The horses had heads like lions, and fire and smoke and burning sulfur billowed from their mouths. One-third of all the people on earth were killed by these three plagues— by the fire and smoke and burning sulfur that came from the mouths of the horses. Revelation 9:15-18 NLT

Now, let's do the math together. Using the present world population of about 8 Billion people, if there is no Rapture until the middle of the Tribulation, one quarter of the population die during the fourth seal judgement alone:

8 billion – 6 billion = 2 billion dead

Then one third of the remainder of humanity is going to die during the sixth trumpet judgement alone:

6 billion – 4 billion = 2 more billion dead

The total is already 4 billion people, half the world population already dead before the middle of the Tribulation. But remember, those are only the deaths from those two judgements alone.

Then, we have to take into account all the other people who will die during all of the other seal and trumpet judgements, which will be anywhere from millions to perhaps another billion and the real picture (the truthful one) of the first half of the Tribulation begins to come into focus.

The truth is that there will be no relatively peaceful, bloodless first half of the Tribulation. Actually, when one adds the numbers up, more people will die from numerous different causes during the first half of the Tribulation (well over 4 billion) than will die during the second half of the Tribulation. The judgements upon the remainder of humanity will just continue to increase in severity after that.

Knowing this about the Scriptures, there is no one on Earth who can convince me that the first half of the Tribulation is not the wrath of God. The first half of the Tribulation is actually going to be horrendous, and the judgements will just keep getting worse after that for those who remain alive and still refuse to repent and follow Christ during the second half of the Tribulation.

It is so important for us to understand that the purpose of the wrath of God is not to torture the godly, but to bring the wicked of humanity to repentance, that they might be saved and not perish eternally, but how many today are really listening?

But the people who did not die in these plagues still refused to repent of their evil deeds and turn to God. They continued to worship demons and idols made of gold, silver, bronze, stone, and wood—idols that can neither see nor hear nor walk! And they did not repent of their murders or their witchcraft or their sexual immorality or their thefts. Revelation 9:20-21 NLT

As In the Days of Noah

There are quite a few Christians today who believe in a

post-tribulation rapture, and they will point to Luke 17 and Matthew 24, where Jesus talks about His second coming and the end of the world (as it now exists) and they will say "SEE! SEE! It says that when Jesus returns at the end of the Tribulation, we'll be 'taken'." Sometimes, even advocates of a pre-tribulation rapture will mistakenly try to use these same Scriptures to suggest that Jesus is talking about the Rapture here, but in this case, the post-tribbers are partly right. These Scriptures are not talking about the Rapture at all.

The first problem is that Jesus cannot be talking about a pre-tribulation Rapture here because in Matthew 24, the question asked by the disciples is not when they would be "caught up" to live with Jesus in His Father's House, but, "What would be the sign of Christ's coming and the end of the world?"(See v.3.) Then Jesus responds by telling them:

The day is coming when you will see what Daniel the prophet spoke about—the sacrilegious object that causes desecration standing in the Holy Place." (Reader, pay attention!) "Then those in Judea must flee to the hills. A person out on the deck of a roof must not go down into the house to pack. A person out in the field must not return even to get a coat. How terrible it will be for pregnant women and for nursing mothers in those days. And pray that your flight will not be in winter or on the Sabbath. For there will be greater anguish than at any time since the world began. And it will never be so great again. In fact, unless that time of calamity is shortened, not a single person will survive. But it will be shortened for the sake of God's chosen ones. Mathew 24:15-22 NLT

So Jesus is giving a message to anyone who comes to Christ during the Tribulation and they somehow manage to stay alive until the Antichrist sets up his image in the temple. Jesus is warning them that they had better take note of that, and flee as far from society as they can possibly get. Why? Because after that, anyone who does not swear allegiance to the Antichrist will certainly be put to death, and those in the cities are going to be the easiest to find and capture, so they will be the ones executed first.

Then Jesus goes on in verse 29 to say that immediately after those days Jesus is going to come to Earth to take over and establish His kingdom, and the Millennium will begin.

Therefore, Jesus is obviously not talking about the pre-tribulation Rapture here. On top of that, we also have to take a close look at who is being "taken" and who is being "left" in Matthew 24. Many have automatically assumed that it is saying Christians will be "taken" in the Rapture at this time, but will it be Christians who are "taken" at this time? The correct scenario is given to us in verses 37-39, where Jesus says:

But as the days of Noah were, so shall also the coming of the Son of man be. For as in the days that were before the flood they were eating and drinking, marrying and giving in marriage, until the day that Noe entered into the ark, and knew not until the flood came, and TOOK THEM ALL AWAY; so shall also the coming of the Son of man be. Matthew 24:37-39 KJV

Therefore we see that Matthew 24 is indeed talking about Christ's return to establish His Kingdom, but just as the wicked were all taken away (destroyed) in Noah's day and the believers were left to repopulate the Earth, so also will it be when Jesus returns to set up His kingdom on Earth. It will be the wicked who will all be taken away (destroyed) and the elect remnant of believers who will remain and go into the Millennium, still in their natural bodies for the purpose of repopulating the Earth again, just as happened in the days of Noah.

There is one more major Scripture passage which is often brought up in the controversy over when the Rapture will occur, and that is in 2 Thessalonians, so let's take a look at it as well:

Now, dear brothers and sisters, let us clarify some things about the coming of our Lord Jesus Christ and how we will be gathered to meet him. Don't be so easily shaken or alarmed by those who say that the day of the Lord has already begun. Don't believe them, even if they claim to have had a spiritual vision, a revelation, or a letter supposedly from us. Don't be fooled by what they say. For that day will not come until there is a great rebellion against God and the man of lawlessness is revealed—the one who brings destruction. He will exalt himself and defy everything that people call god and every object of worship. He will even sit in the temple of God, claiming that he himself is God. 2 Thessalonians 2:1-4 NLT

There are those who use this Scripture to try to suggest that it proves that the Antichrist must come to power and sit in the temple of God in Jerusalem BEFORE the Rapture occurs, not discerning that Paul is talking about two separate events here. First of all, regarding the coming of Christ to set up His kingdom, Paul says that this cannot happen until after the Antichrist desecrates the Temple in Jerusalem, agreeing with everything Jesus said.

Then right after this statement, Paul also reminds the Thessalonians (and us) of what he has already said in I Thessalonians 1 regarding Jesus returning for His Bride (and the Holy Spirit in us) occurring before all of this happens:

Don't you remember that I told you about all this when I was with you? And you know what is holding him back, for he can be revealed only when his time comes. For this lawlessness is already at work secretly, and it will remain secret until the one who is holding it back steps out of the way. Then the man of lawlessness will be revealed, but the Lord Jesus will slay him with the breath of his mouth and destroy him by the splendor of his coming. 2 Thessalonians 2:5-8 NLT

What is it then that Paul has already told us, and WHO is the person who is presently holding back evil and preventing the Antichrist from coming to power? Let's go back to Paul's previous letter to the Thessalonians which also matches what Jesus told His disciples in John 14:1-4. Here, I believe the answer is clearly laid out for all who want to believe it:

For if we believe that Jesus died and rose again, even so God will bring with Him those who sleep in Jesus. For this we say to you by the word of the Lord, that we who are alive *and* remain until the coming of the Lord will by no means precede those who are asleep. For the Lord Himself will descend from heaven with a shout, with the voice of an archangel, and with the trumpet of God. And the dead in Christ will rise first. Then we who are alive *and* remain shall be caught up together with them in the clouds to meet the Lord in the air. And thus we shall always be with the Lord. Therefore comfort one another with these words. 1 Thessalonians 4:14-18 NKJV

So, we see that in 2 Thessalonians Paul is addressing two separate events, the coming of the Lord to set up His kingdom, and our gathering together unto Him in the Rapture, which Paul had already covered earlier in his first letter to the Thessalonians, where Paul had already explained that when Jesus comes to catch us up, God will bring with Him those who are already deceased in Jesus. I hope that helps clarify that Paul was speaking about two separate events, occurring at two different times.

Chapter 11

Ready or Not
The Bridegroom is Coming!

Together, Let's be Ready!
There Will be a Rapture!

Now you know why I believe, according to what I read in the Scriptures, there can be no POST-TRIBULATION rapture of living believers, because all surviving believers at the end of the Tribulation will be going into the Millennium in their natural biological bodies to repopulate the Earth during those thousand years.

You also know that the reason I believe there will be no MID-TRIBULATION rapture is because the Scriptures clearly show us the wrath of God will be poured out on this unrepentant, wicked, and adulterous generation of humanity right from the very beginning of the Tribulation, with billions of people dying (more than half of the human population) well before humanity ever gets to the middle of the Tribulation, and it will keep getting worse as time goes by, all the way to the end,

Yet do not be discouraged. I believe that Christ's "catching up" and removal of believers and the Holy Spirit in us will be a lot like when the water breaks and pours out during a woman's pregnancy. No one knows exactly when that living water is going to break and leave, but once the living water is gone, the real labor pain begins and it is going to continue in frequency and intensity until the new birth occurs.

In this case, when the body of Christ and the Living Water of the Holy Spirit in us leaves in the Rapture, the Tribulation is going to begin and continue until the Kingdom of Jesus Christ arrives - is born into reality on Earth, as it is in Heaven.

If you study the book of Revelation in detail, you will find that the first 3 chapters are pretty well all about the church and warnings to the church to "repent" because judgement is coming. In fact, God warns the churches seven times in the first three chapters of Revelation to "Repent." Then you do not hear anything at all about the church from then on until we return with Jesus to put a stop to Armageddon.

When we take a look at Revelation chapter 4, anyone who has done some study on a pre-tribulation rapture will point out to people that God calling John to "come up" and John's testimony that the 24 elders (the 12 patriarchs of Israel and the 12 Apostles of the church) are ALREADY in Heaven when he gets there presents a very compelling "type" or "shadow" indicating that the coming resurrection of all believers, living and dead will have already occurred by Revelation 4.

Why? In John's vision, when John arrives in Heaven in Revelation 4, the 12 patriarchs of Israel and the 12 apostles are already there before the Judgements of God begin, suggesting that the resurrection and Rapture will occur and believers will be removed from Earth BEFORE the Tribulation begins, with that event not described as happening until later in

Revelation 6.

Throughout all of the judgements of God in the next 16 chapters of Revelation, there is NO mention at all of the church or the resurrection until Revelation 20 when Jesus returns to set up His kingdom on Earth, and God says that those believers who DIED during the Tribulation will live and also become part of the First Resurrection, reigning under Jesus with the rest of us during the Millennium.

Notice that it only mentions that the DECEASED tribulation believers will be raised and join the rest of the resurrected saints at that time. There is no mention at all of a resurrection of LIVING believers occurring at the end of the Tribulation because it is not going to happen.

Those who are still alive will be going into the Millennium to repopulate the Earth, just as Noah and his family did, and those believers and their descendants will be the ones who will be ruled over by Jesus and the Raptured and Resurrected believers during those first thousand years. They will be living in a near-perfect world without Satan, but still susceptible to sin and the possibility of death.

Are We Ready for Christ's Return?

In these closing chapters of this book, let's take a look at some of the Scriptures which I believe are in agreement with God's call to humanity to LISTEN to what the Spirit of God is saying to the churches and the rest of the world in these last days.

We do not know exactly when Father God will send Jesus

to retrieve His Bride and take us to His Father's House, but Jesus wants us to be comforted and have faith that He will be coming to take us to His Father's House, and God wants us to be spiritually ready for our Lord's arrival to claim His Bride at any moment. God does not want us to be troubled by all of the things that are happening in the world around us, but God does want us to be READY for Jesus when He comes:

Let not your heart be troubled; you believe in God, believe also in Me. In My Father's house are many mansions; if *it were* not *so,* I would have told you. I go to prepare a place for you. And if I go and prepare a place for you, I will come again and receive you to Myself; that where I am, *there* you may be also. And where I go you know, and the way you know. John 14:1-4 NKJV

Yes! Jesus said He was leaving Earth to go and prepare a place for us in His Father's House. Why? Jesus tells us why. He is going to come again to RECEIVE us to Himself, that where He now is, we will be joining him and there WE MAY BE ALSO. We know where Jesus has gone. We know the way we will be able to go to where He is. God has told us it will be via the resurrection, or the Rapture (depending on whether we are deceased or still living when He gets here).

What we DON'T know is exactly when that will happen, but Jesus said to make sure we are ready. This means that TODAY is the day for us to repent of our sins and NOW is the time for us to already be living for, and walking with, Jesus Christ.

It will not matter what you or I personally believe about when Jesus is going to return for us if our death occurs before that happens. Regardless of when the Rapture will occur, the reality of life is that people drop dead, or are killed by various other causes every day, and there is no guarantee that any of us will have tomorrow to get right with God if we do not do it now, today.

Many have falsely believed that the Bible parable of the ten virgins in the Bible is talking about those who profess to be Christian and the rest of the world. They think the foolish virgins are those who are not professing Christians. They think they are avowed unbelievers

Yet we know that this is cannot be true because no avowed unbeliever is actually looking for and waiting for the return of Jesus, the Bridegroom. Unbelievers don't believe He is resurrected. They all believe Jesus Christ is dead and buried and that is the last that anyone will see of Him or hear from Him, so they are not the ones waiting for the Bridegroom.

No, the parable of the ten virgins is all about professing Christians who are all waiting and looking for the return of Jesus Christ. There are some who try to insist that when God speaks of the WISE having "oil" in their lamps, God is talking about their particular concepts of receiving or being filled with the Holy Spirit.

There are even some who try to make the foolish suggestion that it is all about those who speak in tongues, declaring that anyone who does not speak in tongues are all going to be left behind. Again, that is not Biblical.

We only have to look at Matthew 25:12 where Jesus says "I don't know you.", and compare that to the words of Jesus earlier in the book of Matthew to have a really excellent understanding of who will NOT be going in the Rapture when it occurs.

"But while they were on their way to buy the oil, the bridegroom arrived. The virgins who were ready went in with him to the wedding banquet. And the door was shut. "Later the others also came. 'Lord, Lord,' they said, 'open the door for us!' "But he replied, 'Truly I tell you, I don't know you.' "Therefore keep watch, because you do not know the day or the hour. Matthew 25:10-13 NIV

Not everyone who says to me, 'Lord, Lord,' will enter the kingdom of heaven, but only the one who does the will of my Father who is in heaven. Many will say to me on that day, 'Lord, Lord, did we not prophesy in your name and in your name drive out demons and in your name perform many miracles?' Then I will tell them plainly, 'I never knew you. Away from me, you evildoers!' Matthew 7:21-23 NLT

Repent and Believe on Jesus!

Jesus could not possibly make it clearer to us. In this translation, He says that the reason many will not go in the Rapture is that they are evildoers. In the KJV, it says that they are "working iniquity," and consequently Jesus has no relationship with them. They do not really know Him, even though they claim to know Him.

When the Bride of Christ is taken up to be with Jesus and the door to Heaven is closed again, it will not do anyone any good to try to argue with God about religious service, good deeds, or claims that "Jesus is Lord." If our behavior is unrepentant and continuing in evil, Jesus says we will not be going with Him, regardless of when the Rapture will occur and how loudly we argue with Jesus that we believe in Him.

Listen to me, brothers and sisters. Please do not grieve the Holy Spirit by trying to say that Christ's teaching of our need to repent is preaching "salvation by works" and we are saved "by grace, through faith". We are indeed saved by God's grace through faith in Jesus Christ and not of works, but "repentance" is not works.

Repentance is **not** trying to become saved by doing good works. "Repentance" is turning away from darkness and honestly asking the Holy Spirit to help us to cease from evil behavior because we know that we cannot be saved if we continue to follow Satan, not even if we claim to be "Christian."

Repentance is not "doing" anything! Repentance is our obedient response to God to STOP doing evil (with the help of God's Holy Spirit). As I have mentioned before, a true definition of the false idea of "salvation by works" is when people continue to be unrepentant and disobedient to God while thinking that our good works, our religious service, our claims to be Christian, and our shouts of "Jesus is Lord" are what will save us.

One of the great mysteries of iniquity is man's determination to believe Satan's same old lie that God's instruction for us to repent, to believe, trust and obey Him is the demand of a cruel taskmaster who is trying to keep something good from us.

Really, if you believe this, you are just believing the same old lies of Satan that He used on Adam and Eve right from the very beginning in the Garden of Eden. "God's trying to keep something good from you. You won't die! You'll become (evolve into) gods if you believe, trust, and obey the Devil and embrace evil instead of listening to God."

Look at where that has gotten us, dear friends. How long will it be before we finally understand that God is calling us to repentance because He loves us deeply and wants to set us free from the evils that are destroying our lives? Together, let us learn to love, trust, and obey God, for that is the only key to a fulfilling life while we are in this world, and eternal life in the world to come.

There are many professing Christians all around the world today whose lives are a total disaster, ruined because someone, somewhere, told them all they had to do was say they believe in Jesus and everything would work out fine.

They were even told that everything was OK between them and God, and now many people, maybe even some of you who are reading this book, have wandered far from God. Maybe you are even blaming God for your ruined lives. Maybe the Devil has even been pushing you toward suicide, telling you that God does not love you.

Don't listen to these voices any more. It is time for many people today to admit that it is because they have never really believed, trusted, and obeyed God, and have been listening to lies that their lives have become so painful and hopeless.

If that is you, dear friend, now is the time to be set free. Now is the day to be honest before God and take responsibility for where your life is at. It is time to start trusting, believing and obeying God so the rest of your life can be a blessing and not a curse. God only wants us to repent for our own good. He takes no pleasure in the death of the wicked. God is not willing for any to perish, but for all to come to repentance, and because of that, God will never reject anyone who comes to Him asking for forgiveness, mercy, and help from the Holy Spirit to follow Christ.

No matter how far we have strayed from God or what we have done, we are all still God's offspring and He wants us back. He wants us to return to Him and be His children again. God's grace and the blood of Jesus Christ is sufficient to cleanse us of all our sins if we just turn around (like the prodigal son) and come back to our Father in Heaven, trusting that Jesus will fulfil His promise to come to take us with Him, so that where HE NOW IS, we can be also.

What if I am Wrong?

One of the most misguided accusations of those who reject the teaching of a pre-tribulation rapture is that, if we are mistaken, we will be the cause of people "falling away" from Christ and being deceived by the Antichrist if the pre-tribulation Rapture does not happen. There are even some who accuse us of preaching "doctrines of demons" that will cause many to lose their salvation when the Tribulation comes and we all have to go through it and suffer.

Really? If you think we believe and teach that our salvation is based on when we think the Rapture is coming, you really don't know us, or our teachings very well. I have always taught, and will say again here that anyone who thinks their salvation is based on their opinion of when the Rapture will occur instead of how they live their lives and who they are following (either Jesus, of the Devil) is definitely on dangerous spiritual ground, playing with fire. We need to listen to what Jesus says.

What we preach is that mankind's salvation is based solely upon how we respond to Jesus Christ when He has called us to repent of our sins and believe on His life, death and resurrection for our redemption. Believing the gospel, we know and trust that on Father God's appointed day, regardless of WHEN it happens, we too will be resurrected (or raptured), and so shall we ever be with the Lord.

We have learned that the most important aspect of our lives is to fully live for Christ NOW, and because it is already our goal and our greatest desire to do that, we are just as prepared spiritually for whatever is coming as any mid or post tribulation believer.

In fact we are much better prepared than any person who has been deceived into thinking that there will be no consequences if they keep working iniquity now while they wait for another "sign" like the building of the Temple in Jerusalem or the rising of "Antichrist" before they decide to truly follow Jesus.

As for me, I will repent of my sins and follow Christ, and if I am wrong about when the Rapture will occur, I have lost nothing and gained everything. The last 40 years of my life with Jesus has been my greatest joy. Likewise, every mid or post tribulation believer (who repents and has that same faith in Jesus) is also already living the best life they can ever live. They are ready for Jesus if He comes when they think He will, and just as ready if Jesus shows up today, so whenever Jesus does come, they will go with Him just as surely as I will.

The only ones who are in great danger today will be any people from all three camps who think that they can keep serving the Devil while claiming to be a follower of Jesus, deceived by false preachers into believing the wicked are going to inherit the kingdom of God. God loves every one of us, but He clearly tells us in His Word:

Say to them: '*As* I live,' says the Lord God, 'I have no pleasure in the death of the wicked, but that the wicked turn from his way and live. Turn, turn from your evil ways! For why should you die, O house of Israel?' Ezekiel 33:11 NKJV

If you have believed nothing else I have told you in this book, dear friend, at least believe this. God loves us deeply and wants us to spend eternity with Him. That is why He sent Jesus to die so we could be redeemed, but the warnings God gave to Israel still apply to Christians today.

If you don't know Jesus as your Savior yet, or if you are a professing Christian, but your life has not gone well because you have not been fully living for God and following Jesus, I hope and pray that this book has been a help to you and you will make that decision to repent and come to Christ NOW, TODAY, and may God's blessing be upon every one of you.

The angels in Heaven rejoice every time a lost child of God comes home, and if you have chosen to repent and follow Jesus Christ today, I know that the Spirit of God Himself is running out with tears to meet you. May the Lord bless you and keep you as you press in ever closer to Jesus, and I encourage you to reach out to give that same gift to others by sharing Christ with others as God opens doors for you to do so.

About the Author

Pastor Michael Hunter is a licensed Christian Minister involved in pastoral and prophetic ministry for 40 years. He has been a member of the Christian Ministers Association of Canada since 1987 and presently functions as an associate pastor at Lake Country Life Center in British Columbia, Canada.

Books by Michael Hunter

If you enjoyed this book and found it helpful, purchase a copy for a friend. All book sales profits fund the ministry as seen at www.crmca.net.

Ask your local bookstore or library for a copy of Michael's books.

Visit www.crmca.net and download the eBooks free!

The story of my own journey back to God.

Who is Jesus Christ?

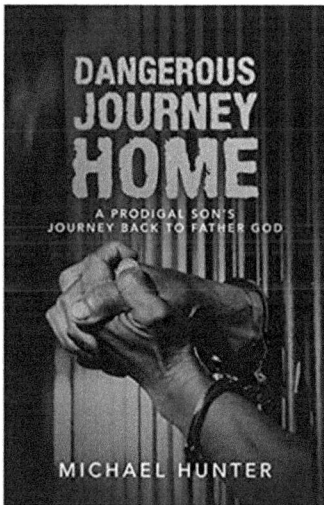

Download Michael's eBooks at no cost: www.crmca.net

www.ingramcontent.com/pod-product-compliance
Lightning Source LLC
Chambersburg PA
CBHW051952090426
42741CB00008B/1358